The Lyrical Bridge

The castle and bridge at Heidelberg.
COURTESY OF VERKEHRSVEREIN HEIDELBERG TOURIST ASSOCIATION.
(See chapter 2)

The Lyrical Bridge
Essays from Hölderlin to Benn

Philip Grundlehner

Rutherford • Madison • Teaneck
Fairleigh Dickinson University Press
London: Associated University Presses

Associated University Presses, Inc.

Cranbury, New Jersey 08512

Associated University Presses
Magdalen House
136–148 Tooley Street
London SE1 2TT, England

Library of Congress Cataloging in Publication Data
Grundlehner, Philip, 1945–
The lyrical bridge.
Bibliography: p.
Includes index.
1. German poetry—History and criticism—Addresses, essays,
lectures. 2. Bridges in literature. I. Title.
PT73.B75G77   831'.009'356   76–46765
ISBN 0–8386–1792–1

PRINTED IN THE UNITED STATES OF AMERICA

To Nora Winay and Hugo Bekker

Contents

Acknowledgments

I would like to thank the following publishers for permission to reprint copyrighted material:

Insel Verlag for permission to reprint material from Rainer Maria Rilke, *Gesammelte Werke, Gesammelte Briefe,* and *Briefe 1902–1906, Briefe 1914–1921.*

Limes Verlag Max Niemeyer for excerpts from Gottfried Benn, *Gesammelte Werke in acht Bänden;* Limes Verlag Wiesbaden und München.

Verlag Heinrich Ellermann KG for permission to reprint the poem "Fahrt über die Kölner Rheinbrücke bei Nacht" from Ernest Stadler, *Dichtungen,* ed. K. L. Schneider (1954).

Schocken Books Inc. for permission to reprint "Die Brücke" from Franz Kafka, *Beschreibung eines Kampfes: Novellen, Skizzen, Aphorismen aus dem Nachlass,* ed. Max Brod. Copyright © 1946 by Schocken Books. Copyright renewal © 1975 by Schocken Books Inc.

Liveright Publishing Corporation for permission to reprint an excerpt from Hart Crane's *The Bridge,* in *The Complete Poems and Selected Letters and Prose of Hart Crane,* ed. Brom Weber. Copyright 1933, © 1958, 1966 by Liveright Publishing Corporation, New York, N.Y.

1

Introduction

Although the bridge has been employed as a significant symbol by a wide range of writers and poets, critical examination tracing its influence has not been extensive. One study, "The Religious Significance of the Bridge,"[1] by C. F. Bleeker, discusses the importance of the bridge in Eastern and Western religious tradition, where it is found to be a universally recurring symbol. Bleeker concludes that the bridge typically allows a flow of communication in two directions—not only does it lead the gods into the regions inhabited by man, but it also provides man accessibility to a celestial kingdom after death. An example of its religious application is found in the Catholic "pontiff," a name for the Pope designating a bridge between heaven and earth, and "pontifex," a member of the supreme college of priests in ancient Rome. A second study, "Railroad, Bridge, Tunnel,"[2] by Rudolf Erckmann, concerns the bridge as a respresentative of man's technical prowess and achievement in the modern age. Erckmann notes the significance of the bridge in literature: "Easily associated with 'bridge' were the notions of triumph over nature and the abysses, of bold venture, man's daring, of perfection, flight, heaven, the all, of the ascent to the divine." In a third article, "The Bridge:

A Study in Symbolism,"[3] Dr. Paul Friedman treats the psychoanalytic importance of the bridge in dreams but alludes only tangentially to its significance as a literary symbol. Friedman observes the influence of the bridge "upon the fancy and fantasies of man" and invites further study regarding its literary significance: "Perhaps the bridge's clearest, creative expression may be found in the works of writers and poets which afford many truly illuminating examples of bridge symbolism. It is remarkable that as one examines these expressions of creative imagination, they seem to offer compelling proof that the author has projected himself into this image." These three studies are sufficient to suggest the universality of the bridge symbol and its interdisciplinary as well as cross-cultural characteristics. Walther Silz, in his detailed study of Hölderlin's "Heidelberg," refers not only to the importance of the bridge in that poem, but alludes to the comprehensive significance of the bridge as a metaphor for poetry and the artistic process itself: "One definition, or emblem of poetry might be: the seeing man on the bridge over the stream."[4]

Because there is so little material available, an extensive study of the bridge symbol is a unique undertaking. Elisabeth Frenzel cites the dearth of motif and symbol studies in general: "Untersuchungen über die Art der Struktur und Funktion von Symbolen und Symbolgeweben liegen bisher nur spärlich vor."[5] This study will not treat the symbol as it is used in such genres as the novel or the novella, both of which will be discussed briefly below, but will be confined to the aspect of the bridge in poetry. The nine poems examined represent only a selection of over one hundred in which the bridge plays a role. Poems where the bridge has little figurative value, such as Gertrud von le Fort's "Deutsches Leid"[6] or David Friedrich Strauss's "Ermunterung,"[7] were not considered. An index provides the reader with the names and authors of some of the poems not discussed. The period of time considered extends from Hölderlin to Gottfried Benn. This period has not been arbitrarily selected since the bridge as a symbol does not exist significantly in poetry before 1800. Before this date it appears only infrequently and without relative importance. The poetry of major authors from the Middle Ages through the periods of the Reformation, Baroque, Enlightenment, and *Sturm und Drang* were researched but yielded little material. Speculation as to why this is so is an interesting topic in itself, but lies beyond the limits of this study.

The bridge as a symbol will be discussed within a comprehensive examination of each individual poem. It will be shown that although the bridge may appear only once in several poems, its significance is such that it becomes the focal point and central symbol of each poem. In order to indicate this significance a full discussion of each poem is needed. The main characteristics of the symbol will be repeated in several chapters to indicate the features common to bridge poetry regardless of the poetic subgenre or literary epoch in which they appear.

The use of the bridge symbol is not limited exclusively to German poetry. An early example in English literature is Wordsworth's "Upon. Westminster Bridge," written in 1802, which expresses the union between man and his creation, the city:

Earth has not anything to show more fair:
Dull would he be of soul who could pass by
A sight so touching in its majesty:
This city now doth, like a garment, wear
The beauty of the morning; silent, bare,
Ships, towers, domes, theatres, and temples lie
Open unto the fields, and to the sky:
All bright and glittering in the smokeless air.
Never did sun more beautifully steep
In his first splendour, valley, rock, or hill;
Ne'er saw I, never felt, a calm so deep!
The river glideth at his own sweet will;
Dear God! the very houses seem asleep;
And all that mighty heart is lying still!

As the city acquires, "like a garment," an anthropomorphic mold and is endowed with the spirit of the musing poet, so reciprocally the poet's soul is expanded to encompass the majesty of the city, "all bright and glittering in the smoke-less air." The meditative poet thus uses the bridge as a symbol of synthesis and accord.

No less expressive of harmony is Hart Crane's 1930 poem *The Bridge*, which seeks to establish a bridge of communication between natural and technological realms and reflect a modern consciousness of unity. According to Crane, an American poet, his bridge becomes "a symbol of our constructive future, our unique identity, in which is included also our scientific hopes and achievements of the future."[8] Crane creates a vision of modern myth as he poetically transforms his bridge from a state of matter into an instrument of the spirit. It not only synthesizes the fragmented world to join city, river, and sea, but figuratively vaults the American continent to reach an inward heaven that is the fulfillment of man's need for order:

> Through the bound cable strands, the arching path
> Upward, veering with light, the flight of strings,
> Taut miles of shuttling moonlight syncopate
> The whispered rush, telepathy of wires.
> Up the index of night, granite and steel—
> Transparent meshes—fleckless the gleaming staves—
> Sibylline voices flicker, waveringly stream
> As though a god were issue of the strings. . . .[9]

Although written more than a century apart, the bridges in both Wordsworth's and Crane's poems represent a point of contemplation and moment of creative flux where seeming opposites can merge into a vision of beauty and unity.

As stated above, this study will concern itself exclusively with the bridge in German poetry. Yet, to enforce the validity of this investigation, a brief view of prose citations of the symbol is necessary. German prose writers of the nineteenth and twentieth centuries utilize the bridge to as significant an extent as do the poets. Representatives include major authors of both centuries and some of their most important works. Goethe, Hoffmann, Nietzsche, Kafka, Mann, and Hesse are among the authors whose prose demonstrates a certain fascination with the bridge symbol.

In Goethe's *Märchen,* for example, the serpent transforms itself into a bridge to become a symbol for commerce and progress as well as love:

> Ein grosser, mit Säulen umgebener Platz machte den Vorhof, an dessen Ende man eine lange und prächtige Brücke sah, die mit vielen Bogen über den Fluss hinüberreichte; sie war an beiden Seiten mit Säulengängen für die Wanderer bequem und prächtig eingerichtet, deren sich schon viele Tausende eingefunden hatten und emsig hin und wider gingen. Der grosse Weg in der Mitte war von Herden und Maultieren, Reitern und Wagen belebt, die an beiden Seiten, ohne sich zu hindern, stromweise hin und her flossen. Sie schienen sich alle über die Bequemlichkeit und Pracht zu verwundern, und der neue König mit seiner Gemahlin war über die Bewegung und das Leben dieses grossen Volks so entzückt, als ihre wechselseitige Liebe sie glücklich machte.[10]

In becoming a bridge, the serpent sacrifices itself for the good of man. Through its love it links the "ugly," prerevolutionary world with the ideal, postrevolutionary world across an abyss of irresponsible politics.

For E. T. A. Hoffmann, in his *Das Fräulein von Scuderi,* the bridge Pont Neuf in Paris serves as the symbolic setting where Scuderi abandons her isolation from the world and takes an active part in solving the mysterious murders plaguing the city. As her glass coach crosses the bridge, a note is given to her that commits her to absolving Oliver of accusations against him. No longer separate from a city diseased with crime and poisonings, Scuderi, the poetess, rejoins society and intervenes to avert catastrophe. The bridge thus becomes one of the central symbols of the story, for through its use Hoffmann intimates that poetry must not be isolated from life but rather committed to healing a suffering world.

The bridge is also a recurrent symbol throughout the works of Nietzsche. In the first part of *Also sprach Zarathustra*, the bridge symbol is used to reflect Zarathustra's decision to communicate his wisdom to others and his resolution to descend from the mountain heights, although he understands that his ultimate quest of perfection will remain unachievable:

> Was gross ist am Menschen, das ist, dass er eine Brücke und kein Zweck ist: was geliebt werden kann am Menschen, das ist, dass er ein Übergang und ein Untergang ist. . . . Ich liebe Den, welcher nicht einen Tropfen Geist für sich zurückbehält, sondern ganz der Geist seiner Tugend sein will: so schreitet er als Geist über die Brücke.[11]

Zarathustra relates that the profoundest experience is to reject happiness, virtue, and pity as justifications for existence. He looks favorably upon the man who considers himself a bridge to something more vital than conventional morality allows. Although exhibiting this vitality may mean his own destruction, Zarathustra understands that chaos is a necessary function of creativity: "Ich liebe Den, dessen Seele übervoll ist, so dass er sich selber vergisst, und alle Dinge in ihm sind: so werden alle Dinge sein Untergang."[12] Many times throughout *Zarathusra* the bridge becomes a metaphor for man's hoped-for transformation into the Superman and his goal of making a new beginning out of innocence and forgetfulness:

> Dort war's auch, wo ich das Wort "Übermensch" vom Wege auflas, . . .—dass der Mensch eine Brücke sei und kein Zweck: sich selig preisend ob seines Mittags und Abends, als Weg zu neuen Morgenröten.[13]

For Franz Kafka, whose novels and stories are also suffused with the symbol of the bridge, such "neue Morgenröte" are few. The enigmatic initial paragraph of *Das Schloss* depicts K.'s first glimpse of the castle from a wooden bridge: "Lange stand K. auf der Holzbrücke, die von der Landstrasse zum Dorf führte, und blickte in die scheinbare Leere empor."[14] The symbol again is one suggesting transition, this time between the explicable world of light and the mysterious, veiled world that shrouds the castle in mist and darkness. The Bridge Inn (*Brückenhof*) subsequently becomes the scene of many confrontations and realizations as K. futilely attempts to penetrate the castle's walls. That K. must cross into a metaphysical realm not experienced in the ordinary world is summed up by Olga when speaking to K.:

> Zwar heisst es, dass wir alle zum Schloss gehören und gar kein Abstand besteht und nichts zu überbrücken ist, und das stimmt auch vielleicht für gewöhnlich, aber wir haben leider Gelegenheit gehabt zu sehen, dass es, gerade, wenn es darauf ankommt, gar nicht stimmt.[15]

The final pages of *Der Prozess* also exhibit Kafka's use of the bridge. As Josef K. is accompanied by the two men leading him to his execution, the group passes over a bridge in the moonlight: "Alle drei zogen nun in vollem Einverständnis über eine Brücke im Mondschein. . . . Das im Mondlicht glänzende und zitternde Wasser teilte sich um eine kleine Insel, auf der, wie zusammengedrängt, Laubmassen von Bäumen und Sträuchern sich aufhäuften."[16] Josef K. pauses for a moment on the parapet to view the idyllic setting and reflect on the bygone days of pleasure and comfort. Crossing this bridge marks his final passage from a carefree life to one of overpowering guilt and finally death. It is not long before Josef K. realises the illusion and the impossibility of sustaining such a harmonious interlude: "Ich wollte ja gar nicht stehenbleiben," he says. As he continues on to the other side of the bridge, the moment of escape is forgotten: "Der eine schien dem anderen hinter K.s Rücken einen sanften Vorwurf wegen des missverständlichen Stehenbleibens zu machen, dann gingen sie weiter."[17]

Similarly in Kafka's *Urteil*, the protagonist Georg, unable to reconcile the incompatibility between himself and his father or between himself and his friend in Russia, jumps off a bridge at the end of the story. That his suicide takes place on the bridge reflects Georg's inability to cope with the "unendlicher Verkehr"[18] representing the world of everyday reality. Whereas the bridge signifies commerce and communication for the normal world, for Georg it is the lack of communication and understanding that precipitates his death.

Perhaps Kafka's most poignant use of the bridge is found in his short sketch "Die Brücke,"[19] where a personified bridge narrates its story in the first person: "Ich war steif und kalt, ich war eine Brücke, über einem Abgrund lag ich." On a summer evening a traveler comes to the uncharted heights where the bridge is situated. After the bridge confidently prepares to support this first human being, it senses the traveler's lightly prodding it with the iron point of his walking stick, and then is shocked to feel him jumping with both feet onto the middle of its structure. Shuddering with pain, the bridge attempts to turn and see who the traveler is: "Wer war es? Ein Kind? Ein Traum? Ein Wegelagerer? Ein Selbstmörder? Ein Versucher? Ein Vernichter?" As it turns to look, the bridge falls into the abyss and is transpierced by the sharp rocks, "die mich immer so friedlich aus dem rasenden Wasser angestarrt hatten." This short tale is as mystifying as it is brief. The bridge, whose support is only "in bröckelndem Lehm" from the beginning, initially has the confidence to support human life and provide safe passage. However, when faced with the reality of a meddlesome and callous representative of mankind, it loses its self-assurance and ability. In the end, the bridge suffers destruction because of its own inquisitive attempt to identify the source of its misery. Had it not made this attempt, the bridge might well have continued its tenuous yet peaceful existence. But as always with Kafka, it is the introspective and analyzing mind that undermines any capacity for maintaining a life of strength and self-confidence. In all of Kafka's stories, the bridge provides only illusory support or a brief romantic spirit of harmony. For Kafka, the bridge thus provides yet another symbol of a world where all traditionally strong and dependable structures and institutions are made ambiguous by hopelessness and despair, and become the *loci* of disaster rather than sustained vitality.

Thomas Mann also makes frequent use of the bridge symbol. When Tonio Kröger returns home after his torrid adventures in the south, for example, he walks across the bridge of the city where he was a child: "Er ging zu Fuss, ging langsam, den unablässigen Druck des feuchten Windes im Gesicht, über die Brücke, an deren Geländer mythologische Statuen standen, und eine Strecke am Hafen entlang."[20] The bridge represents Tonio's transition back to the atmosphere of love and longing that he had experienced before his departure. The mythological statues on the bridge enforce the dreamy atmosphere that was part of his youth before he was subjected to the dichotomy of "icy intellect and scorching sense." The bridge represents a partial reconciliation between these opposites and symbolizes Tonio's arrival at an understanding of his artist's dilemma. Upon passing over the bridge he affirms this reconciliation: "Und diese Gegenwart nun unterschied sich durch nichts von einem dieser betörenden und unzerreissbaren Traumgespinste, in denen man sich fragen kann, ob dies Trug oder Wirklichkeit ist, und sich notgedrungen mit Überzeugung für das letztere entscheidet, um dennoch am Ende zu erwachen. . . ."[21]

The bridge symbol is also frequently employed in Mann's *Tod in Venedig*. As the boat pulls into the Venetian harbor, Aschenbach casts an awestruck glance on the Bridge of Sighs, a symbolic anticipation of his own death. He continually pursues the object of his love, Tadzio, over the bridges of the canals, whose evil exhalations grow stronger as Aschenbach becomes more and more desperate to fulfill his desire. It is on a bridge that he finally loses sight of Tadzio altogether, an incident that causes such exasperation and exhaustion that he must give up the search: "Die Polen hatten eine kurz gewölbte Brücke überschritten, die Höhe des Bogens verbarg sie dem Nachfolgenden, und seinerseits hinaufgelangt, entdeckte er sie nicht mehr."[22] This bridge is the final transition for Aschenbach. From this point onward he is seen only in sitting or lying positions as he slowly acquiesces to the urge to relax and slumber.

Perhaps the most significant use of the bridge for Mann is in his *Zauberberg*. Hans Castorp, determined at first to be just a visitor and not a patient at Davos, decides to take a walk after breakfast one morning, ironically remarking to his companion Joachim, "Wir wollen doch sehen, ob ich nicht ein anderer Kerl bin, wenn ich nach Hause komme."[23] As he ascends the meadow path, he approaches a small wooden footbridge, where he pauses to enjoy the musical sound of the rushing water. It is here that Hans experiences the first overt sign of his inherent illness, a violent and persistent nosebleed, which depletes his strength significantly: ". . . wenn er ausgeatmet hatte, fühlte er lange kein Bedürfnis, neue Luft einzuholen. . . ."[24] The bridge symbolizes Hans's transition from the world of the plains in the north to the disease-ridden atmosphere of the sanatorium. He returns to the footbridge several times through the course of the novel to gaze at the stream and meditate. Each time, he realizes that he has become more acclimated to the mountain atmosphere and more distant from the flat land. As in *Tod in Venedig*, the bridge in *Zauberberg* functions as a symbol of passage to decline and loss of vitality.

For Hermann Hesse, the bridge symbol is seen significantly in two works. In *Demian*, the youthful Emil Sinclair's first meeting with the villain Franz Kromer takes place under a bridge where the flowing river is littered with refuse. The bridge suggests Emil's transition from the domestic "light" world of bourgeois tranquility to the criminal "dark" realm of immorality and physical excess, the figurative litter of which must be experienced before a true discovery of the self is possible. Emil confesses: "Mein Bewusstsein leugnete die empordämmernde neue Welt. Daneben aber lebte ich in Träumen, Trieben, Wünschen von unterirdischer Art, über welches jenes bewusste Leben sich immer ängstlichere Brücken baute, denn die Kinderwelt in mir fiel zusammen."[25] In a subconscious quest for his true self Emil dreamily paints, among other scenes, a picture of a Roman bridge with cypress trees, indicative of his desire to discover the uncharted paths of his personality.

In Hesse's *Unterm Rad*, the protagonist Hans Giebenrath, tortured by the pressure imposed upon him by his elders and school examinations, pauses frequently on the bridge of his hometown, contemplating the beauty of the river, the dam, the willow trees, the mill, the meadow, and the escape they offer. In the last of these meditative vigils he realizes the futility of the structured world of society and envisions his escape into nature, an escape that prefigures his drowning in the river: "Auf der Brücke musste er sich setzen; er war so müde und glaubte, nicht mehr nach Hause zu kommen. Er setzte sich auf die Brüstung, er horchte auf das Wasser, das an den Pfeilern rieb und am Wehr brauste und am Mühlrechen orgelte. Seine Hände waren kalt, in Brust und Kehle arbeitete stockend und sich überstürzend das Blut, verfinsterte ihm die Augen und rann wieder in plötzlicher Welle zum Herzen, den Kopf voll Schwindel lassend."[26] The bridge in this most pessimistic novel of Hesse represents not only a place of reflection, but also Hans's final transition from life to death when he seeks to recover the lost dreams of his childhood by returning to nature through suicide.

These prose examples help to underscore the importance of the bridge as a literary symbol. The following nine essays represent not only some of the major poets of nineteenth- and twentieth-century German literature, but a succession of literary eras, including German Classicism, Realism, Impressionism, and Expressionism. The selected poems reveal a wide and differentiated employment of the bridge symbol. In some, it indicates union or transition between the realms of present and past, life and death, or the physical and the transcendental. In others, it is seen as an entity that separates the poet from his environment or as a meditative vantage from which he can view the surrounding landscape or the flowing water beneath him. A brief view of the poems will introduce these themes.

For Hölderlin, in his poem "Heidelberg," the bridge is a classical symbol. Hölderlin aspires toward a universal tranquility within himself and all that surrounds him. He controls his romantic urge to dissolve his longing heart in nature as the old Heidelberg castle stands as a reminder of his cultural heritage. The conclusion of the poem pictures a balance between man and nature; culture tempers nature and nature embellishes culture. The poet himself stands on the bridge as a synthesis of cultural and natural elements.

Platen's "Wenn tiefe Schwermut meine Seele wieget . . ." employs the bridge to establish his cultural identity with the city of Venice. His disciplined sonnet form evidences an ostensible control over his material, yet the frequent and consistent images of decay reveal a loss of emotional balance and a deterioration of inner vitality. There are no redeeming forces of communication and reciprocation as there are for Hölderlin—only the active "Geist," the poet's creative mind, unsuccessfully attempting to overcome the stagnation within his spirit.

The two poems by Meyer, "Die alte Brücke" and "Auf Ponte Sisto," represent the poet's ability to evoke a panoply of colorful historic events in Switzerland and in Rome and disclose their relation to the present. The bridge in both poems removes the poet from reality and allows him to view and experience a variegated and animated landscape of the imagination.

The bridge of Fontane's ballad "Die Brück am Tay" reflects a supernatural transcendence over a dissonant human realm. Fontane's harmony is found neither in culture nor in nature but in the artistic, mythical sphere that surrounds and subjugates the real world.

Like Platen, Nietzsche also fails to achieve final composure within his soul, even though he is able to create a consummate impressionistic scene in which the poetic vision merges with the Venetian landscape. For Nietzsche, lyric expression is essentially circular and self-destroying.

"Venedig" reveals only a final alienation and the inability of language to reconcile the poet's unstable condition. But in contrast to Platen, Nietzsche is not capable of masking his pain; rather, he ironically exposes it to emphasize his dilemma all the more poignantly.

Rilke, a neoromanticist, is able to retreat entirely within himself and not feel the necessity of emergence into the "wirre Wege" of the outer world. His bridge in "Pont du Carrousel" becomes a symbol of the art that establishes a final symmetry and universal law.

Stadler is also able to avoid the outer world and transcend a superficial technical realm. His symbolic bridge in "Fahrt über die Kölner Rheinbrücke bei Nacht" is aglow with the lights that glorify man and send him on a journey affirming life and death. Through his creative process, Stadler restores not only himself but all men to a sovereign condition. As an expressionistic symbol, Stadler's bridge marks the emergence of man from a limited technical realm to a spiritual rebirth.

Gottfried Benn's "Am Brückenwehr" lacks the messianic purpose of Stadler's poem. He is concerned rather with discovering the transcendent values that will perpetuate him as a poet. His bridge leads to the values of the "neue Macht" —"Form" and "Tiefe"—whose synthesis he achieves in the final "Reigen" image of the poem.

Common to each poet in his use of the bridge is the quest to achieve an artistic sovereignty over that disorder which he perceives confronting him. The bridge thus becomes a symbol for art itself, which harmonizes all dissonant factors of the outside world. It marks the poet's desire for ultimate order and composure. The central question pursued in the essays is how, and to what extent each author is able to attain such harmony. This study does not attempt to trace a systematic development of the bridge motif but rather examines its significance under various conditions by various authors. The nine poems have been selected on the basis of their artistic virtuosity as well as on the richness of association generated by each bridge symbol.

2

Friedrich Hölderlin :
"Heidelberg"

Heidelberg

Lange lieb' ich dich schon, möchte dich, mir zur Lust,
   Mutter nennen, und dir schenken ein kunstlos Lied,
     Du, der Vaterlandsstädte
      Ländlichschönste, so viel ich sah.

Wie der Vogel des Walds über die Gipfel fliegt
   Schwingt sich über den Strom, wo er vorbei dir glänzt,
     Leicht und kräftig die Brücke,
      Die von Wagen und Menschen tönt.

Wie von Göttern gesandt, fesselt' ein Zauber einst
   Auf die Brücke mich an, da ich vorüber ging,
     Und herein in die Berge
      Mir die reizende Ferne schien,

Und der Jüngling, der Strom, fort in die Ebne zog,
   Traurigfroh, wie das Herz, wenn es, sich selbst zu schön,
     Liebend unterzugehen,
      In die Fluten der Zeit sich wirft.

Quellen hattest du ihm, hattest dem Flüchtigen
   Kühle Schatten geschenkt, und die Gestade sahn
     All' ihm nach, und es bebte
      Aus den Wellen ihr lieblich Bild.

Aber schwer in das Tal hing die gigantische,
   Schicksalskundige Burg nieder bis auf den Grund,
     Von den Wettern zerrissen;
      Doch die ewige Sonne goss

Ihr verjüngendes Licht über das alternde
   Riesenbild, und umher grünte lebendiger
     Epheu; freundliche Wälder
      Rauschten über die Burg herab.

Sträuche blühten herab, bis wo im heitern Tal,
   An den Hügel gelehnt, oder dem Ufer hold.
     Deine fröhlichen Gassen
      Unter duftenden Gärten ruhn.

Eins zu sein mit allem, das ist Leben der Gottheit, das ist der Himmel des Menschen. . . . In seliger Selbstvergessenheit wiederzukehren ins All der Natur, das ist der Gipfel der Gedanken und Freuden.[1]

These words evince Hölderlin's desire for a unity of man and nature. Many poems of his later years are concerned with this theme, such as "An den Aether," "Die Eichbäume," "Die Musse," "Der Wanderer," "Der Nekar," "Der Main," "An den Frühling," "Der Winter," and "Heidelberg." All possess a joyfulness and optimism in life despite an abiding awareness of sadness and illustrate Hölderlin's aphorism: "Der hat viel gewonnen, der das Leben verstehen kann, ohne zu trauern."[2]

"Heidelberg," written in 1800, is representative of Hölderlin's nature philosophy. The spirit of the divine, which the poet earlier has sought in the distant past or future, he now finds in the natural beauty of the city and the surrounding countryside. The ode, called by Mörike "das schönste Hölderlinische Gedicht,"[3] celebrates a communion between man and nature, and expresses Hölderlin's gratitude to Heidelberg for revealing to him the unity pervading all life. A study of the images used in the poem will reveal the extent to which Hölderlin integrates the realms of man and nature.

The ode begins with a tribute of love and admiration for the city:

> Lange lieb' ich dich schon, möchte dich, mir zur Lust,
>   Mutter nennen, und dir schenken ein kunstlos Lied,
>   Du, der Vaterlandsstädte
>   Ländlichschönste, so viel ich sah.

An immediate intimacy is established in the *du* address. Although the first two strophes are in the present tense, the poem describes an experience reaching deep into the poet's past. The first and last words of the first strophe, "lange" and "sah" indicate this expanse of time. Hölderlin had visited Heidelberg on three occasions over the twelve years prior to writing the poem,[4] and his verses evidence a final sublimation of thought and feeling. This long acquaintance with and love for the city and the numerous revisions he made in the initial draft[5] do not prevent the poet, however, from expressing the spontaneous feeling that accompanied his inspiration in writing the poem. It relies not on contrived mental processes but is rather a "kunstlos Lied," an artless song based not on ceremony and formality, but on heartfelt and loving intuition. The city, with its many component parts, offers the poet a mirror of the longings that he perceives in his own soul.

This intimacy established in the first strophe between poet and city is nurtured throughout the poem. Heidelberg has sustained, protected, and appeased him to the extent that he chooses it as his metaphorical mother: "möchte dich, mir zur Lust, / Mutter nennen, . . . This desire for familial ties is extended in the third verse with the word "Vaterlandsstadt," which not only completes the parental association of mother and father, but also produces a union between the father "Land" and mother "Stadt." The following word, "ländlichschönste," referring to the natural beauty of the city, is associated with the "land" of "Vaterlandsstädte," and thus the three elements—country, city, and natural beauty—become one composite and inseparable whole. This familial association is consistent with Hölderlin's Diotima, who longs tc place herself in the divine family of nature: "Auch wir sind also Kinder des Hauses, sind es und werden es sein. . . . O nehmt die allesversuchenden Menschen, nehmt die Flüchtlinge wieder in die Götterfamilie, nehmt in die Heimat der Natur sie auf, aus der sie entwichen."[6] In his ode "An den Frühling," Hölderlin refers to "Meine Schwester, die süsse Natur," "Mutter Erde," and "Der Frühling . . . wir nennen dich Bruder."[7] In Heidelberg the poet is able to discover the domestic tranquility and the peace of a long-sought "Heimat."

This introductory stanza functions as a prelude to the poem. It contains the unifying elements to be developed in the subsequent stanzas. The remainder of the fourth verse, "so viel ich sah," refers to the comprehensiveness of the poet's past experience by which he claims to make a judgment on his present state. The use of the past tense also anticipates the enchanted vision of the third through fifth strophes, which commences with "einst."

The second strophe describes Heidelberg more closely and establishes the city's bond with nature:

> Wie der Vogel des Walds über die Gipfel fliegt
>   Schwingt sich über den Strom, wo er vorbei dir glänzt,
>   Leicht und kräftig die Brücke,
>   Die von Wagen und Menschen tönt.

An element of the city, the bridge, and an element of nature, the bird, are brought into comparison. "Sich schwingen," referring to the vaulting bridge, is also associated with the flight of the bird since "Schwingen" are wings or pinions. The treetops ("Gipfel" is Swabian for "Wipfel"[8]) over which the bird flies are compared to the river spanned by the bridge. The image of the bird represents freedom and transcendence, themes that anticipate the divine vision of the subsequent strophe.[9] Hölderlin's "An den Aether" evidences similar symbolism for the bird, which emancipates the poet from his earthbound imprisonment: "Aber des Aethers Lieblinge, sie, die glücklichen Vögel / Wohnen und spielen vergnügt in der ewigen Halle des Vaters! . . . Möcht' ich wandern und rufen von da dem eilenden Adler, / Dass er, wie einst in die Arme des Zeus den seligen Knaben, / Aus der Gefangenschaft in des Aethers Halle mich trage."[10]

The bridge not only is an inanimate object, but by its association with the bird also becomes an organic part of the natural scene depicted: it participates in the final harmony achieved, and the motive verbs of the stanza ("fliegen," "schwingt sich," "glänzt") underscore the activity of human and natural realms as well as their interaction with one another. Not only is the bridge related to nature, but it is itself teeming with the activity of men and wagons. The visual perfection of the landscape is matched by the aural harmony suggested in "tönt." What is normally a cacophony of unblending sounds becomes on the bridge a euphony of musical tones, for not only the poet but all men appear to be integrated into the unity of vision. Hölderlin uses "tönen" similarly in "Der Wanderer" as reflecting human accord:

Lieblich tönt die gehämmerte Sens' und die Stimme des Landmanns,
    Der heimkehrend dem Stier gerne die Schritte gebaut,
Lieblich der Mutter Gesang, die im Grase sitzt mit dem Söhn-lein: . . .[11]

The bridge thus becomes a setting of harmonious interaction as the poet coalesces disparate elements into a unified panorama. The description of the bridge as "leicht und kräftig" reflects the ease and endurance with which man is bound to man and man is bound to nature. As Johannes Klein states, "Die Brücke ist ein gültig gewordenes Symbol des Verbindenden."[12]

The third and fourth strophes move the poem into the realm of personal experience and establish the bridge as the focal point of the scene:

> Wie von Göttern gesandt, fesselt' ein Zauber einst
>   Auf die Brücke mich an, da ich vorüber ging,
>   Und herein in die Berge
>   Mir die reizende Ferne schien,
>
> Und der Jüngling, der Strom, fort in die Ebne zog,
>   Traurigfroh, wie das Herz, wenn es, sich selbst zu schön,
>   Liebend unterzugehen,
>   In die Fluten der Zeit sich wirft.

The previous lines were of a general nature and served to describe the background against which Hölderlin now perceives his own communion with nature. The present tense is changed to the preterite to describe a specific event of past experience. The bridge on which the poet stands becomes an image that fuses the present with the past moment. Previous associations regarding the unifying aspects of the bridge are now transferred to the reflective poet, who is halted and transfixed by the unity of life he observes.

In a moment of reflection the poet is transported into a world apart from the "Wagen und Menschen" of reality. For him the experience is divine: "Wie von den Göttern gesandt." Whereas all else is in motion around him, he becomes the only stationary entity. Having taken leave of all things transitory ("vorübergehen") in a moment of enchantment ("Zauber"), he now reflectively looks at the river below, which glimmers ("glänzt") to beckon his gaze. The poet's physical stasis, however, does not prevent an inner activity of the spirit, for the subsequent strophes reveal a vivacity and animation equal to the physical movement presented in the initial strophes. Thus the bridge not only is symbolic of the union of past and present and man and nature, but also reflects the transition from the real world to a divine realm of subliminal vision.

In the first draft of his poem, Hölderlin reveals an additional motive for pausing on the bridge to praise the city:

> Ach! Da ich müssig und still über die Brücke ging
> Ein vertriebener Wanderer
> Der von Menschen und Büchern floh.[13]

He is fleeing the narrow, philosophical world of Fichte and Schiller that he experienced in Jena. Heidelberg and the manifold beauty of its nature are therefore originally associated with a biographical transition from flight to rest, a transition still evidenced in the flight of the river ("dem Flüchtigen") to the final repose at the end of the poem ("ruhn"). Beck comments: "Wir glauben zu verstehen, warum aus der lebendig gegliederten Harmonie des Stadtbildes gerade die Brücke herausgehoben ist: Sinnbild des Übergangs schlechthin, hat sie auch dem Dichter den Übergang von der Flucht zur Ruhe, von der Irre zum Geborgensein, von der unheimischen Fremde, vom 'Elend' zur Heimat im inneren Sinne geschaffen."[14]

Yet a mere appreciation of nature from his vantage on the bridge is insufficient for the poet, and therefore his final draft incorporates the deepened view seen in the vision commencing in the third stanza. The poet now feels that he must immerse himself totally in nature to absorb its essence. Such an alternative presents itself in the image of the river flowing into the distance. Hölderlin looks into "die reizende Ferne," which promises hope for the future and reflects a possibility of a new arrival. The river is represented as a youth who rushes headlong into the distance seeking all-embracing unity. The poet's heart, metaphorically associated with the river's longing, is described in the oxymoron "traurigfroh": sad because it must leave all that has given it love and security, yet happy because self-surrender

promises Dionysian dissolution and accession to the universal
flux of the all. The poet's heart feels such a surfeit of beauty
in the alluring distance ("sich selbst zu schön") that it would
overflow and willingly surrender itself to "den Fluten der
Zeit" in an effort to become part of the divine whole. Such
willful yet tragic submission is evidenced also in Hölderlin's
"Rhein" and "Nekar" poems.[15] In "Empedokles," relinquish-
ment of the self to Aetna reflects a reconciliation with the
gods:

> Das Leben suchst du, suchst, und es quillt und glänzt
> Ein göttlich Feuer tief aus der Erde dir,
> Und du in schauderndem Verlangen
> Wirfst dich hinab, in des Ätna Flammen.[16]

The bridge on which the poet is standing thus also becomes
a symbol for the passage of man from individuality to loss
of self in a larger consciousness, if he should choose such
an alternative. In the "Fluten der Zeit" the poet is no longer
restricted to one time and one being, but caught up in the
continuum of all times despite the sadness ("traurig")[17]
brought about by the loss of individual identity. This submission of the self is manifested in the syntax and verse
structure of the third and fourth strophes. Both strophes
comprise one complete sentence, beginning with the enchantment of the poet and concluding with his longing for
dissolution in the currents of time. All is said as if in one
breath, in one moment of sublime revelation.

Not only the poet, but also the city appears to submit
itself to these divine, unifying forces:

> Quellen hattest du ihm, hattest dem Flüchtigen
> Kühle Schatten geschenkt, und die Gestade sahn
> All' ihm nach, und es bebte
> Aus dem Wellen ihr lieblich Bild.

Heidelberg seeks to build a harmonious rapport with the
river by giving part of itself, so that something of itself may
be with the river when it reaches its distant goal. It soothes
the Neckar on its long journey with cooling shadows, and

the city's banks gaze after the river, protecting it as well as longing to be part of it. Heidelberg thus becomes a spiritual companion to the Neckar, for its image trembles ("beben") within the river's being. There is a festive spirit shared as the river flows toward its own dissolution, much like the festive spirit present before Empedokles' death. All things of nature are in communion, and nothing remains isolated.

Yet such a joyous picture is not without its somber note, as already suggested in the "traurig" of "traurigfroh." Although the poet in the magic of his vision entertains a romantic image of dissolution, one cannot forget that this magic has also paradoxically "chained" ("fesseln") him to the bridge, making such divine abnegation not only sad but also impossible to realize. The vision of dissolution must remain the metaphor that it is (*"wie* das Herz . . ."), and the "wenn" must remain a condition that is not fulfilled. Examined in this manner the fifth strophe assumes an ambivalent meaning: either the city desires to give part of itself to the river as suggested above, or the city's beauty and charm provides a seductive allurement, serving to inhibit the river in its youthful surge. "Beben" reveals a slower, more reflective movement of the river than the previous exuberance of "fortziehen" and "sich werfen." This same ambivalence is reflected in the paradoxical "traurigfroh," which must be regarded as a statement of man's tragic duality that separates him from the ethereal realm of the gods. Such separation is evidenced in "Die Eichbäume," where the gods reign supreme above the earth, and man, although longing, must be chained ("fesseln"!) to the earth:

Aber ihr, ihr Herrlichen! . . .
Keiner von euch ist noch in die Schule der Menschen gegangen
Und ihr drängt euch fröhlich und frei, . . .
Fesselte nur nicht mehr ans gesellige Leben das Herz mich,
Das von Liebe nicht lässt, wie gern würd' ich unter euch
    wohnen! [18]

Thus the city and its banks can be viewed as an alternative to the "reizende Ferne" in their offer of tranquility ("kühle Schatten"), love ("lieblich Bild"), and nurturing gentleness ("Quellen"). They bring about reflection and self-consciousness in the river and retard its flow into the distance.

The sixth strophe introduces a more explicit element of antinomy into the romantic notion of merging with the all:

> Aber schwer in das Tal hing die gigantische,
>   Schicksalskundige Burg nieder bis auf den Grund,
>   Von den Wettern zerrissen: . . .

The old castle stands as a counter-image to the youthful river, and "aber" introduces an opposing view to that of self-dissolution. Unlike the youthful river, the castle does not relinquish itself to the eternal forces of nature but represents survival despite the weathering forces of history and storms.[19] Unlike the young river, the aged castle is well acquainted with the destructive forces of nature, having suffered deteriorating onslaughts that have conspired to consume it. In contrast to the new, light ("leicht") bridge (built 1788), which reflects man's harmony with man and nature, the castle's age ("alterndes Riesenbild") and heaviness ("schwer") signify a long history of strife and hardship ("schicksalskundig"). Although erosive elements have reduced it to a giant, ruined hulk hanging down into the valley, it nevertheless stands as a monument to the survival of man and his culture.

As a product of man's culture, the castle's decay reflects the necessary suffering of man brought about by nature. Yet such suffering is an organic law of nature, as the youthful Hyperion eventually comes to grasp: "Muss nicht alles leiden? Und je trefflicher es ist, je tiefer! Leidet nicht die heilige Natur? O meine Gottheit! Dass du trauern konntest wie du selig bist, das konnt ich lange nicht fassen. Aber ohne Tod ist kein Leben."[20] According to Hölderlin's "Rhein" hymn, it is man's suffering that gives meaning to the gods and their divine bliss.[21]

Thus an ambivalent conception of nature is portrayed in both the river and the castle. But in both cases there is also synthesis of opposites. For the surging river there is the soothing comfort of the city's banks, and in the case of the castle, the "doch" in the final verse of the sixth strophe initiates the coalescence of extremes. Such synthesis is consonant with the poet's position on the bridge—he is not on either side, but reflectively standing in the middle, synthesizing the disparate and antithetical elements he views. Now the sun soothes and rejuvenates the weathered remains of the castle as it "pours" its youth-giving light into the valley. The liquid qualities ("goss") of the "verjüngendes Licht" are reminiscent of the flowing youthful river. The final synthesis of thesis and antithesis is reflected in the words "ewig," "verjüngend," "alternd." Hölderlin suggests that nature embraces even opposing aspects of life. Korff comments: "Hölderlin sieht Natur und Leben mit allen ihren Gegensätzen als ein Ganzes an, und sein Naturglaube ist fromm genug, um diese Gegensätzlichkeit als höhere Gesetzlichkeit der Natur zu fühen."[22] Thus the decaying castle becomes ensconced in living nature, which benevolently covers its crumbling walls:

> . . . und umher grünte lebendiger
> Epheu; freundliche Wälder
> Rauschten über die Burg herab.

"Rauschten" not only imparts the movement of living nature to animate the giant hulk, but implies an intoxication and celebration countering the destructive characteristics of nature. Thus, as in the following verses from "Der Wanderer," the old castle is made young with the green of nature: "Und das heilige Grün, der Zeuge des ewigen, schönen / Lebens der Welt, es erfrischt, wandelt zum Jüngling mich um."[23] The congeniality of "freundliche Wälder" is now in contrast to the apparent malevolence of "von den Wettern zerrissen."

The final strophe of the poem continues and completes this natural organic process, and the poet finds final repose not in the dissolution of "der reizenden Ferne" but in the streets and gardens that are near to him:

Sträuche blühten herab, bis wo im heitern Tal,
An den Hügel gelehnt, oder dem Ufer hold,
Deine fröhlichen Gassen
Unter duftenden Gärten ruhn.

There is constant downward motion evidenced as all levels of nature progressively interconnect—from the "ewige Sonne" down to the castle and the valley and farther down to the hills, the river banks, and finally the gardens, under which the cheerful streets repose: "schwer hing die Burg *nieder* bis auf den Grund, . . . Wälder / Rauschten über die Burg *herab* . . . Sträuche blühten *herab,* . . . Unter duftenden Gärten. . . ." This cascading, downward direction toward final rest is in contrast to the beginning of the poem, where the direction was upward to the bird flying over the treetops, the bridge vaulting over the river, and the poet gazing up into the mountains. The descending motion parallels the erstwhile desire of the poet "liebend *unter-*zugehen," but does not contain an annihilation of the self, but rather a friendly coexistence of poet and nature between extremes of height and depth in the bosom of the city. This rising-falling motion is similarly evidenced in Hölderlin's "An den Aether," where the poet aspires upward as the "Vater Aether" descends to meet him, thus striking a balance, much as in "Heidelberg":

Aber indes ich hinauf in die dämmernde Ferne mich sehne
Wo du fremde Gestad umfängest mit der bläulichen Woge,
Kömmst du sauselnd herab von des Fruchtbaus blühenden
     Wipfeln,
Vater Aether! und sänftigest selbst das strebende Herz mir,
Und ich lebe nun gern, wie zuvor, mit den Blumen der Erde.[24]

The poet, still standing reflectively on the bridge, observes now the unity of man and nature. The city—its castle and pathways—becomes a living part of the ivy, shrubs, and fragrant gardens constituting nature, yet maintains its identity as part of man's culture. The "duftenden Gärten" indicate an olfactory harmony in addition to the visual and aural harmonies already established. Despite the awareness of sadness ("traurig") and destruction ("von den Wettern zerrissen"), everything finds relation to something else: the shores gaze at the river, and the river reflects their image in return; the streets are "dem Ufer hold" or "an den Hügel gelehnt."[25] All is in symmetry and festive rapport: "freundliche Wälder," "heiteres Tal," "fröhliche Gassen." Such celebration and forgetfulness of pain is also found at the conclusion of "Der Wanderer," where "[ich] der Mühn und aller Leiden vergesse / Heut und morgen und schnell unter den Heimischen sei." The entire image structure of "Heidelberg" is predicated on the dynamic forces joining man and nature on a bridge of union. As Korff remarks:

> Die Schönheit des Bildes liegt gerade in den sanft gleitenden Übergängen von Berg und Tal, Land und Stadt, Vergangenheit und Gegenwart, Ruhe und Bewegung, Nähe und Ferne, in der gefühlsmässigen Einheit dieser Gegensätze, die als Gegensätze nur noch der Verstand bemerkt. . . . Von dem abgetrennten Menschen zur Götterfamilie der Natur gibt es *eine Brücke*: die Sehnsucht, selige Hingabe, die Liebe.[26] (italics added)

The bridge must also be viewed as a product of man's culture: "Die Brücke ist als Kunstwerk, gestaltet nach Leitbildern der Natur, gesehen. . . . Eine solche kultur— wie naturverbundene Brücke ist ein Zeichen, und der Mensch kündigt seinen inneren Zustand an, je nach der Art, wie ihm Brücken gelingen."[27] As a symbol of synthesis, the bridge represents the artist's ability to bring peace and harmony to the dissonant world described in the first draft of the poem. It thus forms a classical symbol of the poet's harnessing the incessant flux of elements that he views beneath him to bring about a final repose and permanence in his work of art. He creates classical order and universal accord by transmuting transient aspects of the scene into an artistic mold of durability. It is in this sense that Walter Silz remarks: "One definition, or emblem of poetry might be: the seeing man on the bridge over the stream."[28]

This final repose and tranquility are seen in the last word of the poem, "ruhn," representing a change to the present tense from the preterite of the previous six strophes. The present tense designates a continuation of the harmony found earlier in "tönt," but also implies a pervasive rest brought about by the past conflict of opposites. Such sentiment as expressed in "ruhn" is echoed by Hyperion: "Versöhnung ist mitten im Streit, und alles Getrennte findet sich wieder.—Einiges, ewiges, glühendes Leben ist alles."[29] The image of the gardens is consistent with this synthesis, for the garden itself is a product of man and nature working together. As Hölderlin relates in his poem "Die Eichbäume," "Aus den Gärten, da lebt die Natur geduldig und häuslich, / Pflegend und wieder gepflegt mit dem fleissigen Menschen zusammen."[30] It is in this context that Hölderlin expresses the domestic picture of love for his figurative mother and father in the first strophe of the poem. Thus the "Flüchtling" finds final rest not in self-relinquishment but among men and in the natural beauty of the city. Such final comfort is similarly offered to the homeless itinerant in Hölderlin's "Der Wanderer":

—Heimatliche Natur! Zärtlichpflegend, wie einst, nimmst du den Flüchtling noch auf. . . .
Mildere Sommer zu dir kehr ich getreuer und weiser,
Friedlich zu werden und froh unter den Blumen zu ruhn.[31]

3

August Graf von Platen:
"Wenn tiefe Schwermut meine
Seele wieget..."

Sonnet 36

From: *Sonette aus Venedig* (1825)

Wenn tiefe Schwermut meine Seele wieget,
Mags um die Buden am Rialto flittern:
Um nicht den Geist im Tande zu zersplittern,
Such ich die Stille, die den Tag besieget.

Dann blick ich oft, an Brücken angeschmieget,
In öde Wellen, die nur leise zittern,
Wo über Mauern, welche halb verwittern,
Ein wilder Lorbeerbusch die Zweige bieget.

Und wann ich, stehend auf versteinten Pfählen
Den Blick hinaus ins dunkle Meer verliere,
Dem fürder keine Dogen sich vermählen:

Dann stört mich kaum im schweigenden Reviere,
Herschallend aus entlegenen Kanälen,
Von Zeit zu Zeit ein Ruf der Gondoliere.

Was ist das Menschenleben, wenn wir es recht bedenken? Ein
unseliges Gemisch von den dunkelsten Träumen und rohesten
Wirklichkeiten, und was ist ein Traum anders, als ein vorüber-
wandelnd Nichts, und was ist die Wirklichkeit anders, als ein
Ding, das in den Schranken der Gegenwart liegt, und was ist
die Gegenwart endlich? Der Stoff zu künftigem Sein, ein in
eiligster Flucht vorbeistreichendes Wesen, das kein Mensch
erfasst, das sich in jeder Minute zur Vergangenheit unwandelt.
Was ist das Leben anders als ein Spaziergang um das ver-
borgene Grab?[1]

These words, written by Graf August von Platen in
1815, evince the poet's characteristic view of life. Such
pessimism pervades his works and often assumes a bitter-
ness reminiscent of Heine—"Es gibt so viel in der Welt,
was mich wünschen macht, dass ich niemals geboren
wäre . . . Die Menschen behagen mir immer weniger. Ich
liebe niemand von allen, die mich umgeben."[2] With the
aloof perception of an artist, Platen looked on society
from the viewpoint of a remote observer: "Ich betrachte
alles, ich beobachte die Menschen und ihre Werke, aber
ich lebe nicht mehr mit ihnen: ich stehe im Parterre statt
auf der Bühne."[3] His isolation from society led him to
withdraw into himself, where he found loneliness and
despair:

Ich bin verschlossen in mich, wie ein Leichnam. . . . Nichts
fühle ich mehr und deutlicher als meinen Unwert. Warum
leben solche Menschen, wie ich, die nichts sind und nichts
sein können? Wenn ich das schlechte Urteil betrachte, das ich

selbst über mich fälle, so schaudere ich, wenn ich daran denke was andere von mir halten mögen. Ich bin eine links angehängte, nichts geltende Null. . . .[4]

Such an expressed futility is also evidenced in Platen's *Sonette aus Venedig*, written in 1825. Although several of the seventeen sonnets breathe peace and inner harmony, others, such as the one to be analyzed, manifest the poet's frustration. "Wenn tiefe Schwermut meine Seele wieget . . ." is the last of the Venetian cycle and reveals the essence of his melancholia and isolation. Although the strict sonnet form would superficially indicate the poet's sovereignty over his inner state, a study of the images in this poem will reveal Platen's inner decay and desolation. The bridges mentioned in the poem (the Rialto and "an Brücken angeschmieget") are images that ostensibly indicate union with the city but in fact serve only to emphasize his alienation and separation from society.

The first quatrain establishes the melancholy isolation of the poet as contrasted to the commercial activity of the city:

> Wenn tiefe Schwermut meine Seele wieget,
> Mags um die Buden am Rialto flittern : . . .

Platen seeks the serenity of the night, which enables him to reflect upon his melancholia in solitude :

> Um nicht den Geist im Tande zu zersplittern,
> Such ich die Stille, die den Tag besieget.

The long vowels of the first verse slow the cadence of rhythm to aurally evoke the poet's morose condition. Disyllabic words further retard this rhythm and produce a monotony that expresses the weariness of the poet's soul: "Wenn tie / fe Schwer / mut mei / ne See / le wie / get." In order to achieve this disyllabic consistency, Platen changes the normally monosyllabic "wiegt" to two syllables: "wieget." The two syllables of "wieget" denote the movement inherent in the meaning of the word (one thinks of a cradle

rocking back and forth) as well as the instability of the poet's
mental condition. Yet the musicality inherent in "wieget"
also reveals the poet's fascination with his melancholy state.
In narcissistic reverie he cherishes his weariness, much as
later in the poem, where he is intrigued by the decay of
the city.

The second verse counteracts the slow, melancholy
rhythm of the first. The preponderance of short vowels
connotes the liveliness and excitement of the marketplace:
"Mags um die Buden am Rialto flittern." The "Buden am
Rialto" represent the commerce and communication from
which the poet wishes to remain aloof. "Flittern" contrasts
with "wieget" in the lightness and buoyancy of its sound.
It evokes a visual image of the glittering, colorful life of the
marketplace.

But Platen is indifferent to such life, as suggested by the
word "mags." The poet remains apathetic to the clamor of
the marketplace, because it promises only diversion and not
fulfillment. He must leave its distraction "um nicht den
Geist im Tande zu zersplittern." "Zersplittern" not only
rhymes with "flittern" of the preceding verse to suggest its
association with life, but also connotes the violent, shattering
forces with which life threatens the creative "Geist." For
Platen, the "Geist" must maintain its autonomy from life in
order to remain productive. Any temptation to dally ("im
Tande") in life will distract the poet from his artistic dedica-
tion. Therefore he must seek stillness and serenity, as Schultz
states, "das ruhende Sein, das ihm grösser als die vielfältige
Lebensbewegung des Tages ist."[5] The final verse restores
the alliterative s sound of the first verse; the distractions
that life proffers have been surmounted and the poet's
reflection continues as though uninterrupted by the second
and third verses. The s sound whispers the stillness that the
poet seeks:

Wenn tiefe Schwermut meine Seele wieget, . . .
Such ich die Stille, die den Tag besieget.

"Besieget" recalls "wieget" of the first verse not only in its rhyme and disyllabic structure, but also in its musicality and the motion it suggests. "Tag" recalls "flittern," associated with the life that the poet now disregards. The last verse represents a return to the poet's quest for peace after the disturbance of verses two and three.

In the second quatrain the poet directs his glance at various aspects of the landscape. His vantages are the many bridges that traverse the canals of Venice: "Dann blick ich oft, an Brücken angeschmieget. . . ." The poet uses the plural ("Brü*cken*") and the adverb "oft" to denote the frequency of his melancholy state, in which he seeks stillness. His use of the plural also suggests an aimless wandering, an indifference already expressed in "mags." The bridge functions as an instrument that joins the separate realms presented in the poem. Not only does it connect the Rialto district with the more isolated areas of the city, but it metaphorically connects the interstice between the clamor of the marketplace and the stillness, between day and night, between joy and melancholy, and finally between "Seele" and "Geist"—life and art.

In the first stanza the poet notes his indifference to the life of modern Venice as represented in the Rialto. Although the Rialto is itself a bridge in Venice lined with small shops ("Buden"), it is a symbol of commercial intercourse between merchant and buyer rather than a link between the poet's inner state and the outer world. He has disregarded this life and now, in the second stanza, is enticed by the moribund, decaying aspect of the city. He becomes fascinated by this decay, which reveals an additional symbolic function of the bridge: it represents a transition from life to death. Platen himself participates in this eroding process. He is not merely standing on the bridge, he is "an Brücken *angeschmieget.*" Not an active, self-motivated being, he shares the inert properties of the bridge on which he stands.

Platen's obsession with decay continues throughout the second stanza.[6] From the bridge the poet observes the quiet ripples of the wavelets below him:

> Dann blick ich oft . . .
> In öde Wellen, die nur leise zittern.

The image of the poet looking into the water has narcissistic connotations: the word "öde," which he uses as an adjective for the waves, actually describes the desolate isolation of Platen's own soul. In Sonnet 35, Platen uses the mirror image for a similar purpose:

> Das Auge schweift mit emsigem Bestreben,
> Als ob zurück in seinem Spiegel bliebe,
> Was länger nicht vor ihm vermag zu schweben: . . .

The waves, "die nur leise zittern," suggest the passivity and stagnation of his inner self. "Leise zittern" and "halb verwittern" in the following verse are in contrast to "flittern" and "zersplittern" of the first stanza, which signified clamorous, colorful life. The rhyme has remained consistent, but, as with the poet on the bridge, the realm has changed from that of life to decay and deterioration. Platen glimpses in the decaying landscape the disintegration within himself —the bridge becomes a symbol of the poet's identification with the dying Venice. The sonnet represents an encounter between two fellow sufferers, the poet and the city, both of whom have left the realm of active life and are now seized by a grandiose deterioration.

The third and fourth verses continue to reveal the poet's inner condition:

> Wo über Mauern, welche halb verwittern
> Ein wilder Lorbeerbusch die Zweige bieget.

The image of the "Mauer" is similar to that of the bridge, except that it represents the division between two realms rather than the transition (i.e., the process of decay) between them. However, the wall itself, like the city, is decaying ("Mauern, welche halb verwittern . . ."). "Halb" suggests the semi-comatose state of the poet: his mind is alive (". . . Um nicht den Geist im Tande zu zersplittern, . . .") in its ability to fashion verse, yet the poet also perceives the deterioration ("verwittern") within himself.

The branches of a wild laurel tree hang over the wall. The laurel alludes to the traditional celebration of artistic achievement in Greek and Roman antiquity. Platen is enticed by the laurel bush, because it represents the art to which he aspires in the midst of decay. The "Geist" of the first stanza, which has shunned life, now finds solace in a background that reflects its own condition. The laurel is an appropriate image from which the poet can project his thoughts.[7] But the plant itself shows deterioration. The laurel bush, normally having straight, stiff branches, is now seen drooping over the wall:

> Wo über Mauern . . .
> Ein wilder Lorbeerbusch die Zweige bieget.

The branches hang down "über Mauern"; they are no longer in the realm of life within the city. They have crossed, like the poet's inner self, into the realm of moribund isolation. The laurel bush is also "wild," suggesting its solitude and detachment from the cultured life of the city. This solitude is enforced by the fact that the laurel bush is a rare sight in Venice—when one sees it, it is alone, surrounded by stone and cement.[8]

If the second quatrain represents the poet's change of view from the life of the Rialto to the decaying beauty of the city, the succeeding tercets provide an expanded view of Platen's isolation and moribund state. Consistent with sonnet form, the tercets are set off from the quatrains by a caesura. The poet now turns his glance from objects in the near vicinity to the unending horizon of the sea:

> Und wann ich, stehend auf versteinten Pfählen
> Den Blick hinaus ins dunkle Meer verliere,
> Dem fürder keine Dogen sich vermählen : . . .

The lonely figure of the poet appears, standing on the posts that support the bridges as well as the city. Just as

Platen seems to be part of the bridges ("an Brücken angeschmieget"), he also appears as an inanimate extension of
these petrified supports ("stehend auf versteinten Pfählen").
"Versteinten" conveys this inert condition reflecting the
death and decay for which Venice is a symbol. "Stehend" is
also significant in suggesting that which is stationary and
without life. This stationary element is enforced by verbs
that have lost their emotive force in participial form ("stehend, versteinten, schweigenden, entlegenen"). The "Stille"
that the poet sought in the first stanza is now achieved in
the whispering s alliteration ("stehend, versteinten") as well
as in the images that evoke only a static condition.

The second verse elicits association of isolation and
death:

> Und wann ich . . .
> Den Blick hinaus ins dunkle Meer verliere, . . .

"Dunkle," describing the sea, evokes the somber mood of the
poet and relates to the darkness he sought in the first stanza.
"Verlieren" in the first tercet connotes the poet's feeling of
loneliness and desolation described already with the "öde
Wellen" of stanza two. But his dilemma has now intensified:
the "Wellen" have become a "Meer," the depth and size of
which imply only futility for the melancholy poet. His
resignation now becomes abandonment, for the sea appears
before him as a symbol of an infinite and irrevocable void.
The sea is no longer symbolically married to the land in an
annual ceremony by the doge;[9] now it is aloof from the land,
reflecting the aloofness of the poet from the life of the city.
Here the symbol of the bridge acquires an additional meaning: it links the glorious past history of Venice and its
festivals to the present, decaying city. There is no longer
union, communication, or celebration either for the poet or
for the city, only gradual deterioration and finally death.
The ver- prefixes of the verbs suggest this passing away and
demise: "verwittern, versteinten, verlieren, vermählen." The
bridge of communion (e.g., the Rialto bridge) now becomes

a negative bridge of decay and isolation as the image structure of the poem emphasizes absence rather than presence
of unifying factors.

The isolation of the third stanza becomes resignation in
the final stanza:

> Dann stört mich kaum im schweigenden Reviere,
> Herschallend aus entlegenen Kanälen,
> Von Zeit zu Zeit ein Ruf der Gondoliere.

The poet has attained the tranquility he sought at the
beginning of the poem. The alliterative *s* sound in the
first stanza ("Schwermut . . . Seele, . . . Such . . . Stille . .
besieget") associated with the melancholy solitude of the
poet is now restored. "Dann *s*tört mich kaum in *s*chwei-
genden Reviere. . . ." He is no longer disturbed by the
enticement of life, the "Ruf der Gondoliere." Yet the serenity
Platen has achieved is not a comforting serenity. It is rather
a momentary compromise that he accepts as an alternative
to his inner dilemma. The phrase "Von Zeit zu Zeit," then,
refers not only to the sporadic calls of the gondoliers, but
also to the recurrent periods of depression when the poet
reflectively seeks an answer to the meaning of existence
(this recurrent melancholia was already evidenced with
"dann blick ich *oft*, an Brüc*ken* angeschmieget"). But there
is no answer and Platen must reconcile himself to a passive
acceptance of his situation. The "Wenn . . . dann" statements
encompassing the first two stanzas and the "wann . . Dann"
contained in the tercets express ostensibly a relationship of
cause and effect, but in fact they produce no effect but to
leave the poet in a continued state of limbo. The logical
balance inherent in this condition / conclusion structure is
reflected in the balance of the verb "wieget" in the first
verse. It is no progressive motion, however, but rocking
movement that leads nowhere. Such movement accurately
describes the aimlessness and ennui of the poet's mind.

The "schweigenden Reviere" again echoes the poet's

solitude and alienation from life. The normal human activity implied in the word "Reviere" (a district or quarter) is here negated with silence—an allusion to the poet's rejection of life in the first stanza. Similarly, the "entlegenen Kanälen" in the second verse reflect the poet's remoteness and distance from the noise ("herschallend") and excitement ("flittern") of life. The canals, which form a network of arteries throughout the city, allow commerce and symbolize the communication that Platen repudiates ("*entlegenen* Kanälen"). The "Ruf der Gondoliere," a call that summons one to life and community, is treated as indifferently by the poet as in the first stanza ("Mags um die Buden am Rialto flittern"). Platen remains as isolated from life as the island of Venice from the mainland of Italy.

The isolation and decay that Platen portrays in this poem are expressed abstractly with symbols and metaphors rather than as a direct personal experience. The poet attempts to disguise his emotions with a veil of objectivity. In this respect the poem attains a classical character. Platen uses representative images and is careful to avoid conceits that would betray his personal psychological predicament. His metaphors are typical rather than individualized. As Klein comments,

> Grösser als alles Einzelne soll der künstlerische Geist sein, der es bewältigt und zu einem Ganzen zusammenfasst. Nur das Typische, das Stellvertretende erscheint. Nur so, in einer vollendeten Form glaubt der Klassizist dem Gegenstand gerecht zu werden; und die sinnenhafte, baukünstlerische Leistung, die wir Venedig nennen, ist ja aus bedeutenden geistigen Voraussetzungen entstanden.[10]

These representative images appear throughout the poem and include: "Buden am Rialto," "Brücken," "öde Wellen," "Mauern," "wilder Lorbeerbusch," "versteinten Pfählen," "dunkle Meer," "schweigenden Reviere," "entlegenen Kanälen," "Ruf der Gondoliere."

Yet Platen is not successful in conveying a classicist's impression of Venice. He is never able to exclude his personal *ich* from the objective images that he creates. His subjectivity and reflection continually obtrude beneath the plasticity and abstraction of his images and therefore undermine his classic devotion to beauty.

The poet attempts to disguise his inner insecurity through art: "Eine Mauer trennte ihm Leben und Kunst . . . Heimatlos in der Wirklichkeit, suchte er seine Heimat in den Gefilden des Geistes."[11] Like the baroque poets, he sought to reconcile the confusion of his own life by devotion to form and composition, and poetry becomes for him a quasi *l'art pour l'art* pursuit. He himself emphasized the artist's necessity to subjugate life to art: "Das Genie ist angeboren und geht dem Leben voraus, die Kunst muss gelernt werden und ist die höchste Aufgabe des Lebens für den, der Genie besitzt."[12] But the reader is not deceived by Platen's dispassionate aestheticism, for his poem reveals that the coolness and harmony of the disciplined sonnet form is only gesture and mask for inner dissolution. The stringency of his form only betrays the intensity of his inner dilemma. Hans Lewald remarks:

Die höchste Selbstverleugnung des Künstlers und das Selbstvergessen, wonach er mit der strengen Form strebt, um sich von seinem Zwiespalt zu befreien, wird ihm ungewollt immer zum geistigen Selbstbildnis, weil die Kunst nur eine andere Erscheinung des Lebensgesetzes ist. Von seiner Spannung kann er sich also nicht erlösen, und je mehr er danach trachtet, um so eher bricht die Disharmonie seines Inneren durch die erstrebte Harmonie der Form, der jene verdecken soll. Die Form straft ihn Lügen, wenn er sie leidenschaftlich zu erzwingen versucht.[13]

The decadence he views in Venice is only a reflection of the decadence that he feels within himself:

Platen versucht seine Zerrissenheit zu verbergen, und das führt folgerichtig zur Erscheinung der Krise im Gedicht selbst, in die Gefahr der Spannung und des Gegensatzes von Gehalt und Gestalt; denn jedes Kunstwerk spiegelt ehrlich das Wesen seines Schöpfers, auch gegen dessen Absicht, wider.[14]

Form becomes a type of self-discipline to retard the destructive forces that Platen feels within himself.[15] Yet his tragic inward dilemma breaks through all attempts to veil it with form and objectivity, and in this sense his poetry becomes genuine confessional lyric. Thus the symbol of the bridge represents in the final analysis the passage from objectivity to subjectivity, not subjectivity to objectivity as Platen had hoped. As Klein confirms, "Die Objektivität ist eben Schein, denn Platen verbirgt, indem er offenbart—offenbart, indem er verbirgt."[16]

4

Conrad Ferdinand Meyer:
"Die alte Brücke"

Die alte Brücke

Dein Bogen, grauer Zeit entstammt,
Steht manch Jahrhundert ausser Amt;
Ein neuer Bau ragt über dir:
Dort fahren sie! Du feierst hier.

Die Strasse, die getragen du,
Deckt Wuchs und rote Blüte zu!
Ein Nebel netzt und tränkt dein Moos,
Er dampft aus dumpfem Reussgetos:

Mit einem luftgewobnen Kleid
Umschleiert dich Vergangenheit
Und statt des Lebens geht der Traum
Auf deines Pfades engem Raum.

Das Carmen, das der Schüler sang,
Träumt noch im Felsenwiderklang,
Gewieher und Drommentenhall
Träumt noch im Felsenwiderklang,

Du warst nach Rom der arge Weg,
Der Kaiser ritt auf deinem Steg,
Und Parricida, frevelblass,
Ward hier vom Staub der Welle nass!

Du brachtest nordwärts manchen Brief,
Drin römische Verleumdung schlief,
Auf dir mit Söldnern beuteschwer
Schlich Pest und schwarzer Tod daher!

Vorbei! Vorüber ohne Spur!
Du fielest heim an die Natur,
Die dich umwildert, dich umgrünt,
Vom Tritt des Menschen dich entsühnt!

"Ich möchte mir das Reden ganz abgewöhnen, ich möchte wie die Natur in lauter Zeichnungen sprechen."[1] This desire to form pictures from words, expressed by Goethe, is raised to a higher level in the poetry of Conrad Ferdinand Meyer. His work reflects the wish to fashion symbols in order to create a universal language.

Meyer's many visits to the Alpine mountain regions of Switzerland were the inspiration for much of his nature poetry.[2] The poet could feel a unity with nature not experienced in the city. His sister Betsy talks of her brother's "Fähigkeit sich in das Leben und Weben der Natur traumartig zu versenken. In solchen Stunden fühlte er sich mit ihr verwandt und glaubte sogar bis auf einen gewissen Grad an ihre bedeutsamen Winke und Vorzeichen, an das Omen."[3]

"Die alte Brücke," written and published in 1869 and revised several times before achieving final form in 1882, was included in the section "In den Bergen" of Meyer's collected poems. It expresses his ability "sich traumartig in das Leben und Weben der Natur zu versenken" and his conviction that life is reflected symbolically in nature.

The first stanza contains an element of this dreaminess that pervades the entire poem. As the poet observes the bridge, his attention is drawn to its age:

> Dein Bogen, grauer Zeit entstammt,
> Steht manch Jahrhundert ausser Amt; . . .

"Grauer Zeit" suggests the indistinct and shadowy past that shrouds the bridge's existence. It evokes the fantasy characteristic of the poem and anticipates the historical panorama delineated in the following stanzas. The vagueness of "grauer Zeit" and "manch Jahrhundert" contributes to the timeless quality of the bridge. It has stood from time immemorial and continues to stand as a monument for all ages. The arch is initially emphasized ("Dein *Bogen* . . ."), because it has provided strength and ensured the bridge's longevity. It metaphorically provides the basis of support from which Meyer constructs his poem. Although the bridge has long since become obsolete for utilitarian purposes, it lives on in its symbolic value for the poet. This value is evidenced in the immediate intimacy established in the *du* form of address ("*Dein* Bogen . . . *Du* feierst . . .").

The illusionary character of the old bridge is contrasted in the third and fourth verses by reference to a new bridge:

> Ein neuer Bau ragt über dir;
> Dort fahren sie! Du feierst hier.

It is described as a "Bau," a construction, that accomplishes the pragmatic purpose of supporting traffic ("Dort fahren sie! . . ."), but does not have the dreamy, timeless value of the older structure: "Das neue Bauwerk trägt den Verkehr, während das verfallende dämmert im Traum des Geschichtlichen dahin."[4] This contrast is emphasized by the alliterative associations juxtaposing the two bridges: *B*ogen/*B*au, *f*ahren/*f*eierst. Like the new bridge, the old bridge also supports life, but life that is celebrated in stillness and beauty. "Fahren" indicates only movement and transportation: it is more prosaic in contrast to "feiern," which evokes repose and solemnity—the solemnity that instills a reflective attitude in the poet and induces him to ponder the bridge's significance. The exclamation point ("dort fahren sie!") suggests the haste and excitement with which life passes over the new bridge. Whereas the new bridge symbolizes transitory time, the old bridge symbolizes all time. Its arch has borne the weight of many years and linked the centuries. The last verse contrasts the bridges syntactically: the adverb-verb-subject order of "Dort fahren sie!" is reversed in describing the old bridge: "Du feierst hier." The final "hier" not only presents a contrast to the "dort" of the new bridge, but also describes the nearness of the poet to the old bridge and designates the area to be described in the following stanzas. The span of time represented by the bridge is great, but the space in which events occur is small (there is further reference to this smallness in the "engem Raum" of the third stanza).

The second stanza completes the structure of the old bridge with the mention of the street over the arch: "Die Strasse, die getragen du. . . ." Each element of the bridge contributes significantly to the overall symbolism conveyed. This street over the arch does not teem with traffic as does the new bridge; it too bears life, but life as represented by the growth of nature: "Die Strasse . . . / Deckt Wuchs und rote Blüte zu!" This picture of nature is not merely decorative, but it becomes vividly animate through word associations: "Wuchs" not only designates the greenery and weeds that cover the bridge but is also associated with "wachsen," which indicates the organic growth inherent in the scene. Similarly, "rote Blüte" not only refers to the red flowers adorning the bridge, but is suggestive of red blood which sustains life. By this token, the bridge and its arch take on an anthropomorphic quality; the poet does not address the bridge with *du* only because of familiarity with what it represents, but also because he visualizes the bridge as an organic being. The phrase "grauer Zeit entstammt" in the first stanza suggests a natural organic origin rather than a construction ("Bau") as seen in the new bridge. Similarly, the sentence "Du feierst hier" implies an animate being, one resting after a day's work, rather than a utilitarian structure. The arch "carries" the street ("Die Strasse, die getragen du, . . ."), and the naked, lifeless stone of the bridge is no longer visible but is covered with blossoming life: "Die Strasse . . ./ Deckt Wuchs und rote Blüte zu!" The entire scene is suffused with nature, and all is drawn into a celebration (another meaning of "feiern!") of organic life. The colorfulness of the green plants and red flowers embellishes this scene and helps to blot out the grayness of the bridge's past. The excitement inherent in this triumph of nature is evidenced by the exclamation point at the end of the second verse. It is this natural, organic aspect of the bridge that absolves it of man's intrusion in the last stanza.

The final two verses of the second stanza introduce the mist that surrounds the bridge and saturates its moss:

> Ein Nebel netzt und tränkt dein Moos,
> Er dampft aus dumpfen Reussgetos: . . .

The mist obscures the clarity of the natural picture: the present gradually fades into the past as the mist issues forth from the raging waters beneath and enshrouds the bridge in a veil. The grayness associated with the encroaching mist recalls the "graue Zeit" of the bridge's origin. This penetration of mist is reflected in the subtle intensification of verbal meaning: at first the mist moistens the moss and then soaks and saturates it: "Ein Nebel *netzt* und *tränkt* dein Moos. . . ." Meyer shows a slow, natural transition from the real world of the present to the historical, past world of dreams. The bridge, itself a part of nature, becomes a symbol of this transition between present and past. In the final verse of the second stanza the mist steams up from the river cascading through the Reuss gorge:[5] "Er dampft aus dumpfem Reussgetos: . . ." The sound of "dampft" combined with "dumpfen" reproduces the turbulence ("Getos") of the waters below.[6] Thus there is an aural element enhancing the visual impression already conveyed in the poem. Meyer follows a principle of his friend and mentor Friedrich Theodor Vischer: "Der Dichter wird der Natur ein Auge geben, dass sie geistig blicke, und einen Mund, dass sie rede."[7]

Another poem by Meyer, "Nicola Pesce,"[8] describes a

diver who has forsaken the world and retreated to a dream kingdom in the depths of the ocean. The water purifies him by providing an element in which he can immerse himself and become a part of nature.[9] The old bridge too has left the real world and is saturated by the fog representing the world of dreams:

> Das Wasserreich bringt erlösende Kühle und entrückt der Welt, lässt aber das Erleben zum Traum verblassen. . . . Emil Staiger und Heinrich Henel sind sich einig, dass hier der Dichter wie sonst nirgends in seinem Eigensten zu fassen sei. Kühle Ruhe und sinnendes Träumen ist der wahrste Klang Meyers Werk.[10]

Thus the bridge becomes a symbol of the link between the real world and the intangible world of dreams.

This world of dreams is fully achieved in the third stanza:

> Mit einem luftgewobnen Kleid
> Umschleiert dich Vergangenheit
> Und statt des Lebens geht der Traum
> Auf deines Pfades engem Raum.

Like former images in the poem, the "luftgewobnen Kleid" veils the bridge and imparts a lifelike quality to it. "Luftgewoben," describing the encroaching fog, pictures the cloak of illusion that surrounds the bridge and anticipates the "Traum" in the third verse. It marks the transition from the fog that can be seen by the eye to the dream that can be seen only in the imagination. For Meyer, this transition is a natural process accomplished by a combination of fog and air ("*luft*gewoben"). A garment is woven from the air, which brings both the poet and the bridge back into the "graue Zeit" of the past. This weaving process recalls Betsy's reminiscence about her brother: "Er hatte die Fähigkeit sich in das Leben und *Weben* der Natur traumartig zu versenken." Figuratively, it is the poet's own imagination that is reconstructing, "weaving," events of the past. In order to illustrate this process Meyer creates a garment to clothe what is abstract and intangible. "Umschleiert" is consistent with "Kleid" and "-gewoben," because it conveys not only an idea but a picture which can be visualized and is therefore all the more vivid. The "um" in "umschleiert" implies that the transition from reality to dream, initiated by the gradual penetration of the fog, is complete. The spirit of the past permeates the entire scene.

But this dream world is not a final world for Meyer, as suggested by "schleiert": it is only an imaginary world where reality is momentarily veiled and indistinct but nevertheless immanent. Meyer is not a romantic, for he never entirely loses sight of the real world. But in visionary moments such as this one he was able to combine reality and dream, and symbolized the union of these realms with the bridge. As Heinrich Henel notes,

> The dreams which Meyer describes are complicated by the fact . . . that both the subconscious and the conscious mind are active in them. They resemble the moment just before waking up when reality intrudes upon the sleeper's visions, when he tries to 'get a grip on himself,' and when he is painfully aware of two worlds. And just as the sleeper wants to sink back into oblivion but also struggles to rouse himself, so Meyer wanted both to merge in his dream life and to break away from it.[11]

Meyer's "teacher" Vischer remarked upon this desire to coalesce the real and the imaginary:

> Eigentlich gefällt es mir so ganz doch immer nur da, wo es traumhaft aussieht. Freilich doch auch im Deutlichen, Klaren. Aber beides kann sich ja gut vereinigen.[12]

These two realms of reality and dream are juxtaposed in the third verse. The "Leben" refers to the life that normally traverses the bridge. It is "Leben" in the sense of the everyday traffic and commerce alluded to in the function of the new bridge: "Dort fahren sie!" But the old bridge has a visionary rather than a utilitarian function: it evokes a view of the past that everyday life does not allow. Although its path is narrow ("engen Raum"), this dream nevertheless reveals a multitude of past events in the following stanzas. It is like a baroque mirror-cabinet, which, though small, prismatically reflects many different views of the room in which it stands. One object is reflected differently, depending on the angle and level of each mirror. The narrowest room appears augmented, multiplied in a hundred different aspects. So too with the dream on its narrow path: within it is contained the potential for the revelation of every aspect of life. Here again Meyer uses concrete images to express abstract concepts: the dream is given substance by tangibly placing it as a wanderer ("geht der Traum") on the narrow path of the bridge.

The first three stanzas of the poem form a prelude for the review of historical events that follows. With the fourth stanza the present tense changes to the preterite, whereupon a panorama of past events is portrayed. This structure is similar to the *Rahmenerzählung* technique that Meyer employs in his novellas. It enables him to view life indirectly and obliquely and therefore in greater perspective than an interpretation of present circumstances allows. Witkop remarks: "Ein rückschauender Geist sucht in historischer Betrachtung den verhaltenen Anteil am Leben, den die Wirklichkeit bald überreiten würde."[13] Many types of people and many different epochs are manifested in this historical vision,[14] indicating its scope and potential as well as providing the poet with a deeper understanding of the present world.

This view of the past commences with the goliards who passed over the bridge singing their Latin songs during the Middle Ages:

> Das Carmen, das der Schüler sang,
> Träumt noch im Felsenwiderklang . . .

The melody of this song has not been erased by time, but still echoes from the surrounding cliffs. The rhyme of "sang" and "klang" emphasizes its continued presence. It is not, however, an audible melody, but one that is dreamily evoked in the poet's inner senses (*"träumt* noch im Felsen-wiederklang"). The imaginary song of the past is thus made concrete, and past is united with present by the association of sound reverberating between the cliffs. These cliffs are a part of nature, and nature transmuted through the poet's imagination reproduces the past.

This echo of musical harmony is not the only sound elicited from the past. Also present are sounds of urgency and tension:

> Gewieher und Drommetenhall
> Träumt und verdröhnt im Wogenschwall.

These loud, unharmonious sounds recall the crashing of the "Reussgetos" in stanza two. The neighing of horses suggests an element of turmoil and commotion contained in some violent event of the past. The horses as well as the resonance of trumpets ("Drommetenhall") evoke the tumult of an ancient battle. These sounds too are reflected in nature. They are echoed in the surging waters ("Wogenschwall") of the canyon below.

"Wogenschwall" suggests the swell and turbulence representative of "Gewieher und Drommetenhall." It is in contrast to the more musical connotation of "Felsenwiderklang." The melody of the carmen continues to resonate ("träumt *noch*"), whereas the loud, alarming sounds that are conjured up quickly vanish ("träumt und verdröhnt"). The stanza thus anticipates the conclusion of the poem, where all the events of history are reconciled with nature, and peace and harmony return. Meyer uses nature as a tool to artistically demonstrate the contrasts of life. He is "weaving" a vision of the past by selectively imparting details to nature.

The fifth and sixth stanzas describe a colorful procession of people who have crossed the bridge:

Du warst nach Rom der arge Weg,
Der Kaiser ritt auf deinem Steg,
Und Parricida, frevelblass,
Ward hier vom Staub der Welle nass!

Du brachtest nordwärts manchen Brief,
Drin römische Verleumdung schlief,
Auf dir mit Söldnern beuteschwer
Schlich Pest und schwarzer Tod daher!

Not only the lower classes of the "Schüler" and the "Söldner" are portrayed, but also nobility (Parricida) and the emperor. This variety of people and classes is presented to evoke a kaleideoscopic pageant of history.

Yet, aside from the scholars who sing their carmen, Meyer depicts a negative view of humanity. The bridge itself assumes a pejorative connotation in that it must share the guilt of the reprobates, such as the murderer Parricida[15] and the scandalous Roman emperor, who have crossed it. Mercenaries have used the bridge to carry their plunder across the Alps: ". . . Auf dir mit Söldnern beuteschwer. . . ." It becomes the focal point between north and south[16] and has thus experienced a cross-section of humanity that has passed over it ("Du brachtest *nordwärts* manchen Brief . . . Du warst *nach* Rom der arge Weg.")

The final verse of the sixth stanza ". . . Schlich Pest und schwarzer Tod daher," denotes the physical manifestations of man's crimes, as well as relating the infamous role the bridge plays in transmitting the plague from country to country. It is consistent with Meyer's attempt throughout the poem to render abstract concepts (wickedness, calumny) in concrete terms (plague, the black death). *"Schwarzer* Tod" visually represents the death that accompanies these criminals and mercenaries.

However, this "schwarzer Tod," which signifies man's association with evil, is counterbalanced by the colorfulness of the historical pageant passing in review. Just as the disturbance of the neighing horses and the resounding trumpets is contrasted with the songs of the scholars, the dark side of humanity is countered by the majestic multitude of figures.

Much as the "Gewieher und Drommetenhall" is swallowed by the waves and disappears, so in the final stanza the parading figures of history have vanished. The bridge is absolved of man's intrusion:

> Vorbei! Vorüber ohne Spur!
> Du fielest heim an die Natur,
> Die dich umwildert, dich umgrünt,
> Vom Tritt des Menschen dich entsühnt.

The bridge and its abiding quality, as symbolized by the strength of its "Bogen," remain after the men and events have dissolved. The animation evoked in the poet's vision gives way to peace and harmony.

This alternating process of movement and cessation is a principle of Meyer's art. He maintains that literature depends on motion for its effect: "Bewegung—sei es der unaufhaltsame lyrische Herzensdrang, sei es der epische Wanderschritt, sei es das sturmbewegte Segel dramatischer Leidenschaft—ist und bleibt die wesentliche Schönheit aller Dichtung."[17] Meyer's sister comments on the motion observed in the waters under the *Teufelsbrücke*, which was the inspiration for "Die alte Brücke":

Am 11. Juli 1869 haben wir herrliche Gänge gemacht, oft nach den Wasserfällen und schroffen Felsparthieen der Teufelsbrücke, wo wir dem kühnen Sprunge der Wasser, in der *Mannigfaltigkeit ihrer Bewegung*, dem Rauschen und Stäuben einmal stundenlang bewundernd zuschauten.[18] (Italics added)

Yet this movement is finally balanced by the repose and tranquility of nature, in the reflective stillness of "feiern" as expressed in the first stanza. Helene von Lerber states:

In der Natur sah Meyer nicht nur Bewegung, sondern auch Ruhe, nicht nur Kampf, sondern auch Frieden, nicht nur Not, sondern auch schmerzloses Dasein. Er wusste, dass Spannung und Entspannung in ihr in fortwährendem Wechsel ablösen. Aber dass ein solcher Rhythmus vorhanden ist, dass auf die Spannung immer wieder die Entspannung folgt, das zu wissen und sich dieser Bewegung nun auch hinzugeben, war für ihn Wohltat und Trost. Und deshalb bedeutet die Natur in Meyers Leben und Dichtung—vorab in der lyrischen—in erster Linie Beruhigung und Stille.[19]

The final stanza leaves the momentary realm of pageantry and dreams and returns to the reality of the present world: "Vorbei! Vorüber ohne Spur!" "Vorbei!" refers not only to the expired events of the past, but also to the vanished moment of the dream. Yet in this moment the poet has been able to grasp the symbolism of the bridge and arrives at a deeper understanding of life. The bridge represents a uniting not only of past and present, of dream and reality, but also of nature and poet. Meyer based his symbols on these visionary moments. As Linden remarks:

> Das Symbol beruht auf den schnellen und oft widrigen Verknüpfungen des Traumes; Gleichsetzungen finden statt, die nur für den Augenblick des starken Gefühles gelten können und dann wieder verfliegen.[20]

The bridge thus reverts to the natural elements surrounding it. The use of "fielest heim" is consistent with Meyer's view of nature. "Fielest heim" does not have the connotation of decay or deterioration, but rather the bridge's simple regression to its "Heim"—the natural state from which it evolved in the gray and distant past. "Umwildert" connotes this natural state, which overcomes and absorbs man's work of culture formerly associated with the bridge. "Umgrünt" designates nature's victory over man's interference, whereby natural green coloring overcomes the blackness of death ("*schwarzer* Tod" in the preceding stanza). "Umwildert" and "umgrünt" also recall "umschleiert" in the third stanza, but now the present world of nature rather than the past realm of dreams encompasses the bridge.

Nature absolves the bridge of man's calumny: "Vom Tritt des Menschen dich entsühnt!" It is the new structure that now carries men. The colorful types and classes of people presented in the vision are juxtaposed to modern humanity with the general and colorless term "Menschen." "Rote Blüte" also contrasts with the drab "Menschen" who cross the newer bridge. For the old bridge there are no different types and no class distinctions anymore: it is exonerated from one and all. The specific vocabulary used to describe this absolution ("entsühnt") has religious connotations. But Meyer deviates from traditional Christian standards and reapplies Christian terminology in a secular framework. No longer Christ, but nature, redeems. As Henel comments:

> What Meyer needed was purification and sanctification, the immediate and personal experience of the divine. He found them in solitude, particularly in solitary communion with nature, when he listened to the inner voice and contemplated the awesome marvel of the created world. His was the religion of immanence, a conviction that the divine is immanent in this world and need not be sought in a Beyond or a Hereafter.[21]

It is in this context that "rote Blüte" in the second stanza implies the redemption found in Christ's blood. However, "rote Blüte" is secularized and refers to the natural beauty that redeems the bridge.[22] Nature assumes a similar religious connotation in other poems by Meyer, such as "Himmelsnähe":

> . . . Bald nahe tost, bald fern der Wasserfall,
> Er stäubt und stürzt, nun rechts, nun links verweht,
> Ein tiefes Schweigen und ein steter Schall,
> Ein Wind, ein Strom, ein Atem, *ein Gebet*!
>
> Nur neben mir des Murmeltieres Pfiff,
> Nur über mir des Geiers heisrer Schrei,
> Ich bin allein auf meinem Felsenriff
> Und ich empfinde, dass Gott bei mir sei.[23]
> (italics added)

In nature Meyer is able to find "die Ruhe und Harmonie des Unvergänglichen."[24] This harmony "tönt als tiefster Grundklang seiner Dichtung durch, und liegt in der Erfahrung begründet, dass alles mit den übrigen vergangenen Dingen zu einer einzigen 'friedvollen Macht' verschmilzt, in der auch jede Schuld aufgehoben ist."[25] This harmony is achieved in Meyer's poetry through the use of the symbol, such as the old bridge, which renders in concrete terms that which is abstract or intangible. Such use of the symbol displays affinities to the classical tradition:

> Symbol ist die Beziehung eines Inneren durch ein Äusseres, eines Seelischen durch ein Körperliches, eines Abstrakten durch ein Konkretes. So ist es die Brücke, die die Gegensätze der Welt, Geist und Materie, vereinigen will—in dieser Tendenz zur Harmonie liegt das klassische Moment.[26]

This "klassische Moment" is likewise seen in the harmony that Meyer observes in nature:

> Die Mythen der alten Griechen sind aus der Natur herausempfunden und wirken daher klar und verständlich. Die Geister der Felsen, Bäume und Gewässer drücken ihr Wesen aus und gehören ihnen zu. Sie sind uns vertraut und befreundet. Die klassische Natur beruht auf einem tiefen ursprünglichen Einklang, einer vollkommenen Harmonie.[27]

In writing "Die alte Brücke," Meyer was striving to emulate the clarity and objectivity of classical poetry:

> Dass die Bergwelt, besonders in seinem lyrischen Werk, einen grossen Raum einnimmt, ist begreiflich, weil ihm hier das Grosse, Wuchtige, Gestaltete, Klare in seiner reinsten Form entgegentrat . . . deshalb rang Meyer darum, alles Verschwommene, allzu Romantische seines Wesens abzulegen, um ganz 'wirklich' zu werden.[28]

This attempt to achieve classical realism is evidenced by the lack of the first person in "Die alte Brücke." Although the poem relates a personal experience, Meyer avoids any mark of individuality in his form and the universal scope of his images—his are "überpersönliche verallgemeinerte Sinnbilder."[29] Hence Meyer mitigates his subjectivity in devotion to artistic form: "Meyer hatte die Aufgabe seine Leidenschaft zu verhüllen durch die Mittelbarkeit der Form und durch ihre klare Umrissenheit."[30] The life that he experienced was through art, as evidenced in the envisioned historical procession of the poem. Meyer found real life, as represented by the new bridge, colorless and uninspiring; it is on the old bridge that life becomes vivid and profound. The bridge therefore becomes a symbol of the transition from art to life:

> Nicht durch das Leben war er zur Kunst gekommen, sondern durch die Kunst zum Leben. Die Kunst hatte ihm die Möglichkeit gegeben, das Leben, das ihm in seiner unmittelbaren Gewalt unerträglich gewesen wäre, von sich abzurücken, es nicht mehr ruhlos und fordernd, sondern still und bildhaft zu sehen. Sie hatte ihm die Möglichkeit gegeben, von seiner grünumbuschten Höhe aus betrachtend, ohne sich in sein dunkles Gedränge zu mischen, ohne sich in die Verlorenheit der Erlebnisse zu wagen, die seine zarte Natur zertrümmert hätten. Sie hatte ihm die Möglichkeit gegeben, nicht in der stürmenden, wühlenden Gegenwart, sondern in der beruhigten klaren Vergangenheit zu leben.[31]

Yet the life represented is hardly objective life, though Meyer does aspire toward a classicist objectivity. It remains rather a product of his poetic fantasy, much as he has "woven" nature to create an artistic tapestry. Just as real life holds no interest for Meyer, life as represented through art has no sustained presence for him: his dream is soon "Vorbei! Vorüber ohne Spur!" In the end Meyer is left alone, like the old bridge, solemnly reflecting upon his detachment from art as well as life. One therefore senses that the poet is talking to himself and establishing his own sanctuary in nature when he says, "Dort fahren sie! Du feierst hier."

5
Conrad Ferdinand Meyer: "Auf Ponte Sisto"

Auf Ponte Sisto

Süss ist das Dunkel nach Gluten des Tags! Auf dämmernder
  Brücke
    Schau' ich die Ufer entlang dieser unsterblichen Stadt.
Burgen und Tempel verwachsen zu *einer* gewaltigen Sage!
    Unter mir hütet der Strom manchen verschollenen Hort.
Dort in der Flut eines Nachens Gespenst! Ist's ein flüchtiger
  Kaiser?
    Ist es der "Jakob vom Kahn", der Buonarotti geführt?
Gellend erhebt sich Gesang in dem Boot zum Ruhme des Lieb-
  chens.
    Horch! Ein lebendiger Mund fordert lebendiges Glück.

The natural setting of "Die alte Brücke" is replaced by a
Roman scene in Meyer's "Auf Ponte Sisto." The poem was
written in 1882, some eighteen years after the poet left
Rome, and represents one of his many spiritual returns to

the city. Unlike "Die alte Brücke," the present poem utilizes the first person to describe the events depicted, and as such there is a more personal and direct correspondence established between the poet and the bridge symbol that he utilizes. The reflective poet now stands on the bridge and looks out toward the river bank and the city, as well as down at the Tiber flowing under him. The bridge is not described as in "Die alte Brücke," but functions as a meditative stance from which he creates his work. The bridge is thus not the subject of the poem but nevertheless the major image upon which his lyrical description is based.

The first sentence of the initial verse reveals the polar opposites of darkness and light, which evoke the mood of the poem. Darkness for Meyer, however, is no lugubrious romantic notion of melancholy and solitude, but rather a pleasant and sanguine relief from the glowing heat ("Gluten") of the day. As evidenced by the exclamation point terminating the sentence, the darkness is a time for excitement and not somber reflection. "Süss" thus reflects the poetic enchantment and anticipated joy to be found during the course of the poem. Yet, as revealed in the next verse, it is not total night. As in other poems, Meyer's most favored time occurs during the hours joining day with night. "Schwarzschattende Kastanie," "Auf dem Canal grande," "Die tote Liebe," "Hohe Station," "Gespenster," "Alte Schrift," "Zwiegespräch," and many other poems indicate the poet's predilection for this transitional period between light and darkness.

It is significant that the bridge on which the poet is standing is not frozen in time but is caught in the evanescence of the twilight hour. It appears to be fading in the sunset ("dämmernde Brücke"), and is losing the definition of its structure. Thus it is not a static image but one that itself appears in transition. As the bridge image implies movement from one sphere to another, Meyer chooses an appropriate symbol for his own condition. As we learn in the following verse, although he appears to be stationary on the bridge, the poet chooses to emphasize the movement of his eye along the bank of the Tiber. The bank marks the transition between the city and the river, the two elements that will be the subject of the poem. Consistent with these images of movement and transition is the traditional designation of Rome as an eternal city ("unsterbliche Stadt"). It has no point of termination but lives on in a continuum of time.

Having revealed the inherent movement and changing focus of his vision, Meyer proceeds to describe the elements of the city. His eye falls upon the castles and temples along the bank of the Tiber. Like the bridge, however, these buildings are not discrete and tangible forms. Rather than existing as static monuments, they appear to be involved in a metamorphosis of coalescence and synthesis: "Burgen und Tempel verwachsen zu *einer* gewaltigen Sage." Just as in "Die alte Brücke," where the mists of the ravine obscure the clarity of the bridge's definition, the twilight engenders a merging of otherwise disparate elements. The two spheres implied by the "Burgen und Tempel," seats of earthly and spiritual activity, are now combined ("verwachsen") and unified. No longer do they exist in reality but are transmuted into a literary context, a "gewaltige Sage." Meyer's italicization of *"einer"* in the text indicates his emphasis on this unity. As the poem progresses, there is a process of intensification that stresses the fantasy of the poet's imagination and leaves behind the bland objects of reality. The bridge, the city, the castles, and the temples are all drawn into the creative process and acquire intangible qualities. The poem captures the moment of transition, a figurative, temporal bridge, from objectivity to something more sweet ("Süss"), more mighty ("gewaltig"), and more immortal ("unsterblich") than the burning clarity of day ("Glühen des Tages") could ever offer. The objects of reality become muted in a fusion where their prosaic characteristics are lost and their poetic qualities are assumed. It is only this literary process, this mighty saga, that has the power to forge heterogeneous elements into a poetic unity.

As the poet's sovereign eye moves along the bank seeking

to transform the objects it views, it rests on the torrent
moving below the bridge. The transition between reality and
fantasy now takes place, and the river represents the flux
of the poet's creative vision. No longer is he subject to the
glowing embers of the sunlight, but now is soothed by the
cool, aquatic medium of the river. "Unter mir" not only
describes the proximity of the Tiber to the poet but figuratively represents his penetration of the depths within
himself.[1] With this expansion of the poet's creative consciousness, treasures are revealed to him that were invisible
to the world of light. The poetic fantasy revives the forgotten
wealth of treasures sunken in the depths. "Hort" is thus
understood as the treasure of the imagination, the richness
of fantasy, as well as Meyer's fond memories of Rome, which
are immersed yet accessible to the dreaming poet. In his
chapter "Hidden Treasure," Heinrich Henel comments
regarding the *Hort* motif in Meyer's works: "What would
not let him rest was the consciousness of the treasure he
carried within him. The riches of the imagination, the visions
of the contemplative life demand realization no less
imperiously than the projects of the man of action, and
they demand submission of those who are chosen to realize
them."[2]

The first four verses of the poem are descriptive. The
poet relates his intermediary condition—his position on the
bridge, the impending darkness of evening, the bank of the
river—all of which function as a prelude to his vision, which
comprises the final four verses of the poem. If his fantasy
can truly attain the treasures to which he alludes, there
must be not only description but actual evocation. The
second half of the poem therefore does not merely relate
but, as in "Die alte Brücke," comes alive with a succession
of pictures that animate the poet's "gewaltige Saga" with
immediacy and vitality. Meyer's sister Betsy quotes her
brother regarding his passion for poetic vividness and his
dissatisfaction with mere description: " 'In der Poesie muss
jeder Gedanke sich als sichtbare Gestalt bewegen. Es darf
kein Raisonnement, nichts gedankenhaft Beschreibendes als

unaufgelöster Rest übrig bleiben. Es muss alles Bewegung sein und Schönheit!'"[3]

The "Hort" concluding the descriptive part of the poem is followed by the "Dort" commencing the final visionary section. Thus a bridge of rhyme is created between tangible and intangible realms to effect a smooth transition and to focus the listener's attention on the river below. The excitement of this vision ("Dort in der Flut eines Nachens Gespenst!") parallels the poet's initial excitement at the twilight scene evidenced at the outset of the poem ("Süss ist das Dunkel nach Gluten des Tags!"). But now the vision is significantly intensified. The words comprise only a fragmentary sentence, an ellipsis without verb, indicating the emotion of the speaker's words. "Flut" also appears as a more energetic term for the river than "Strom," suggesting the flood of inspiration that now seizes the poet. "Gespenst" supports the intangible nature of Meyer's vision, since physical objects have long since dissolved their tangible characteristics.

More specific images follow as the poet's vision intensifies into a staccato series of questions. As in "Die alte Brücke" a historical panorama passes in review, bearing out the veracity and vivacity of the "gewaltigen Sage" mentioned earlier. The fleeing emperor enforces the urgent quality of the vision, and "ist's," an abbreviation, once more adds to the syntactical hastiness of the verse. The second image, that of Jakob vom Kahn, enhances the heroic element traditionally part of the saga. Master "Jakob vom Kahn" transported a group of people over the Tiber in the 1530s between Ponte Sisto and Saint Angelo.[4] But again, such events take place not in reality but through the veil of art. Buonarotti, Michelangelo's surname, is mentioned as having been in the boat navigated by Jakob vom Kahn. The artistic saga that Meyer creates in his poem is thus related to the artistic context of Michelangelo. Betsy Meyer talks about her brother's Roman experience as being largely influenced by the work of Michelangelo: "Nun kam er nach Rom und sah die Sistina Michel Angelos. Diese Kunst traf ihn wie ein

Lichtblitz. Buonarotti erschien ihm in seinen Schöpfungen als der grösste Poet. . . . Er wollte jetzt in den Sinn und Gehalt der Dinge eindringen, ihn in sich aufnehmen, bis er in seiner Seele lebendig würde, in sein eigenes Wesen überginge."[5] The question "Ist er der 'Jakob vom Kahn', der Buonaritti geführt?" is then an evocation of the historical and artistic richness of Rome in the early sixteenth century.

The series of questions indicates the wealth of possibilities inspired by the poetic vision. All boundaries, all defining limits, are suspended as the poet allows his creative imagination full sovereignty. The final image of the poem tells of a lover singing tribute to his beloved: "Gellend erhebt sich Gesang in dem Boot zum Ruhme des Liebchens." The verse appears to offer a solution as to the identity of the phantomlike apparition passing in the bark below ("eines Nachens Gespenst!"). No longer is there a question, but rather a final statement as the images of history yield to the eternal image of love, and the past is brought into the present. The richness of the visual stimuli in the poem is now enhanced by aural qualities. Culminating in "Horch!", these qualities comprise the counterpart of the visual "Schau ich . . ." in the second verse of the poem and overcome the queries of the poet. The song not only functions as an additional sense impression to animate the vision but also suggests the song of the poet arising ("erhebt sich") in the twilight to sing praise to his own beloved, the undying city of Rome and the treasure it offers. Such a contention is supported by Meyer's "Trennung von Rom,"[6] written in 1864, which sings a paean of love to the city and acknowledges the "reichen Hort" that he will bring back to his homeland:

> Nun lass mich scheiden, Stadt der Welt, von dir
> Und lass mich dein gedenken, früh und spät,
> Dass die Betrachtung tätig werde mir
>   Und ruhig meine Tat.
>
> Den Ernst des Lebens nehm' ich mit mir fort,
> Den Sinn des Grossen raubt mir keiner mehr;

Ich nehme der Gedanken reichen Hort
Nun über Land und Meer.

The fact that the song in "Auf Ponte Sisto" is shrill and piercing ("gellend") reflects a new pitch of excitement and intensity, as previously evidenced in the poem's syntax and punctuation. "Horch!" represents the zenith of this excitement and amounts to an adjuration to the listener to participate in the poet's elation. As Henel remarks, "the love song asserts the right to happiness, and to disrespect and forgetfulness, of those even who live in the shadow of a majestic past."[7]

The last verse, "Ein lebendiger Mund fordert lebendiges Glück," evidences the result of the poet's creative vision. Through evocation in his mind's eye he has achieved what he feels to be life. If Henel's judgment is valid—that for C. F. Meyer "poetry is unlived life"[8]—this poem is the quintessential example. That which Meyer has not found in reality, in the "Gluten des Tags," he discovers in the treasure within himself, in his own ability to create an inner life. Thus the "lebendiger Mund" in final analysis is the living mouth of the poet, who achieves vital happiness through his own song. Indeed, such vision not only brings about, but demands ("fordert") happiness. Pleasure thus becomes the imperative and the fruition of searching within the self and finding "manchen verschollenen Hort" in the stream ("Strom") of memory and the subconscious. With "Glück" we are taken back again to the beginning of the poem, to the word "Süss" which initiated the poet's vision at the twilight hour. His enjoyment of the scene is now consummated. The symbolic bridge, as in "Die alte Brücke," not only has given him pause to contemplate the unity found within, but has also allowed him to experience it for an enrichment that the torment of active living could never provide.

Twelve years after leaving Rome, Meyer wrote what might be called the companion piece to the later "Auf Ponte Sisto." The same elements are present—the mysterious half-light, the bridge, the eternal city, the flowing of the Tiber, the capitulation of the clamorous daylight hours, the unity of scenery, the metamorphosis of reality into dream, and the rejuvenation to new life of that which was thought to be the hidden, inert past:

Römische Mondnacht (1870)

Ein feierliches Mondenlicht ergiesst
Sich auf das schlummernde, das ew'ge Rom,
Kein Laut, und unter stillen Brücken fliesst
Des heil'gen Tibers unerschöpfter Strom;
Was sich erbaute sein Gestad entlang
Und was zerfällt in Trümmer voller Pracht,
Verwächst in ruhigem Zusammenhang
Zu einer ernsten, friedevollen Macht.

Wie Wellen schweben Ungemach und Glück
Vorüber, keine gleitet mehr allein,
Verschüchtert tritt das laute Heut zurück
In seiner Schwestern leise zieh'nde Reihn;
Die Stunde schämt sich ihrer Ungeduld,
Wo still Jahrtausend an Jahrtausend ruht,
Und es versinkt des Tages Hast und Schuld
In eines grossen Lebens stete Flut.[9]

But this poem was written twelve years before "Auf Ponte Sisto." The theme and component images anticipate the final poem, but "Römische Mondnacht" does not contain the vividness, the flux of elements, and the kinetic historical process found in "Auf Ponte Sisto." Neither is the bridge made the focal point and central symbol of the poet's position between two worlds—of reality and dream. Betsy specifically comments that her brother divided "Römische Mondnacht" into two parts, whereby the first section became "Auf Ponte Sisto" and the second section "Chor der Toten." What were thoughts and reflections in the former poem became animated figures in the latter: "Der Eindruck . . . lebte grösser und mächtiger in ihm auf. . . . Die Gedanken darin wurden zu Personen."[10] It was not until twelve years later that Meyer could adequately translate the rich symbols of his dream life into poetic reality and find the security and support that the bridge over the Tiber could offer him and the vivid figures of his inner self. In the natural setting of "Die Felswand," it is the small suspension bridge over the abyss that offers him a similar comfort:

> Feindselig, wildzerrissen steigt die Felswand.
> Das Auge schrickt zurück. Dann irrt es unstet
> Daran herum. Bang sucht es, wo es hafte.
> Dort! über einem Abgrund schwebt ein Brücklein
> Wie Spinnweb. Höher um die scharfe Kante
> Sind Stapfen eingehaun, ein Wegesbruchstück!
>
> Fast oben ragt ein Tor mit blauer Füllung:
> Dort klimmt ein Wanderer zu Licht und Höhe!
> Das Aug verbindet Stiege, Stapfen, Stufen.
> Es sucht. Es hat den ganzen Pfad gefunden,
> Und gastlich, siehe, wird die steile Felswand.[11]

Although the setting is in the Alps rather than in Rome, the bridge is in both cases a metaphor for the artistic process, which offers a secure path over the abysses and confusions of existence. In both poems it becomes an extension of the inner eye of the poet, which surveys the landscape to combine disparate elements into unity and happiness. Much like the bridge, the artist's inner eye "verbindet Stiege, Stapfen, Stufen. / Es sucht. Es hat den ganzen Pfad gefunden, / Und gastlich, siehe, wird die steile Felswand."

The Rialto Bridge, Venice, during the Historical Regatta.
COURTESY OF ENTE PROVINCIALE PER IL TURISMO, AZIENDA AUTO-
NOMA SUGGIORNO E TURISMO, VENICE. PHOTO GARDIN *E. P. T.*
VENICE. (See chapter 3)

The Cologne Cathedral and the Hohenzollern Bridge.
Courtesy of Hermann Classen Lichtbilder GDL, Cologne.
(See chapter 9)

The Devil's Bridge over the Reuss Gorge, Switzerland.
COURTESY OF THE SCHWEIZERISCHE VERKEHRSZENTRALE, ZÜRICH.
(See chapter 4)

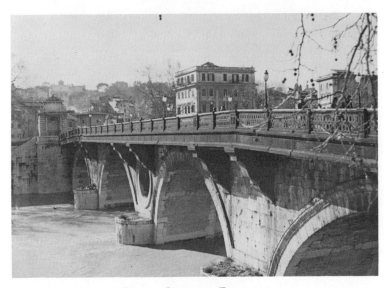

Ponte Sisto in Rome.
COURTESY OF ENTE PROVINCIALE PER IL TURISMO, ROMA. PHOTO
BY E. P. T. ROMA: (See chapter 5)

6

Theodor Fontane: "Die Brück am Tay"

Die Brück am Tay

28. Dezember 1879

"When shall we three meet again?"

(Macbeth)

"Wann treffen wir drei wieder zusamm?"
"Um die siebente Stund, am Brückendamm."
"Am Mittelpfeiler."
　　　　"Ich lösche die Flamm."
"Ich mit."
　　　　"Ich komme vom Norden her."
"Und ich vom Süden."
　　　　"Und ich vom Meer."
"Hei, das gibt einen Ringelreihn,
Und die Brücke muss in den Grund hinein."
"Und der Zug, der in die Brücke tritt
Um die siebente Stund?"
　　　　"Ei, der muss mit."
"Muss mit."
　　　　"Tand, Tand
Ist das Gebilde von Menschenhand."

Auf der Norderseite, das Brückenhaus—
Alle Fenster sehen nach Süden aus,
Und die Brücknersleut ohne Rast und Ruh
Und in Bangen sehen nach Süden zu,
Sehen und warten, ob nicht ein Licht
Übers Wasser hin "Ich komme" spricht,
"Ich komme, trotz Nacht und Sturmesflug,
Ich, der Edinburger Zug."

Und der Brückner jetzt: "Ich seh einen Schein
Am andern Ufer. Das muss er sein.
Nun, Mutter, weg mit dem bangen Traum.
Unser Johnie kommt und will seinen Baum,
Und was noch am Baume von Lichtern ist,
Zünd alles an wie zum heiligen Christ,
Der will heuer zweimal mit uns sein—
Und in elf Minuten ist er herein."

Und es war der Zug. Am Süderturm
Keucht er vorbei jetzt gegen den Sturm,
Und Johnie spricht: "Die Brücke noch!
Aber was tut es, wir zwingen es doch.
Ein fester Kessel, ein doppelter Dampf,
Die bleiben Sieger in solchem Kampf.
Und wie's auch rast und ringt und rennt,
Wir kriegen es unter, das Element.

Und unser Stolz ist unsre Brück;
Ich lache, denk' ich an früher zurück,
An all den Jammer und all die Not
Mit dem elend alten Schifferboot;
Wie manche liebe Christfestnacht
Hab' ich im Fährhaus zugebracht
Und sah unsrer Fenster lichten Schein
Und zählte und konnte nicht drüben sein."

Auf der Norderseite, das Brückenhaus—
Alle Fenster sehen nach Süden aus,
Und die Brücknersleut ohne Rast und Ruh
Und in Bangen sehen nach Süden zu;
Denn wütender wurde der Winde Spiel,

Und jetzt, als ob Feuer vom Himmel fiel,
Erglüht es in niederschiessender Pracht
Überm Wasser unten . . . Und wieder ist Nacht.

"Wann treffen wir drei wieder zusamm?"
"Um Mitternacht, am Bergeskamm."
"Auf dem hohen Moor, am Erlenstamm."
"Ich komme."
            "Ich mit."
                    "Ich nenn euch die Zahl."
"Und ich die Namen."
                "Und ich die Qual."
"Hei!
    Wie Splitter brach das Gebälk entzwei."
            "Tand, Tand
Ist das Gebilde von Menschenhand."

"Die Brück am Tay" is representative of the elder
Fontane's ballads and poems. They are either "Gelegenheits-
gedichte" or poems based directly on newspaper accounts,
and as such rely on reported material rather than invention
for their stimulus. On the night of December 28, 1879, the
center superstructure of the railroad bridge over the Firth
of Tay in Scotland became dislodged during a violent
storm, with the result that an approaching train bound from
Edinburgh to Dundee plummeted into the depths of the
inlet. With over one hundred people killed, only twenty-six
of whose bodies were found, the accident was the worst rail
disaster of the century. The tragedy was publicized throughout the world, leaving many incredulous and alarmed that a
structure of such technical skill and sophistication could fail.
The bridge had been completed just one year prior to the
disaster and was considered a marvel of engineering
advancement—3,250 meters long, 20 meters high, and supported by 81 piers. The structure had cost over seven million
francs and two full years' labor. A newspaper account in the
Zürcherische Freitagszeitung of January 2, 1880, reported as
follows regarding the disaster:

England. Während eines furchtbaren Windsturmes brach am 29. nachts die grosse Eisenbahnbrücke über den Taystrom in Schottland zusammen, im Moment, als der Zug darüberfuhr. 90 Personen, nach andern 300, kamen dabei ums Leben; der verunglückte Zug hatte nämlich sieben Wagen, die alle fast voll waren, und er stürzte über 100 Fuss hoch ins Wasser hinunter. Alle 13 Brückenspannungen sind samt den Säulen, worauf sie standen, verschwunden. . . . Bis jetzt waren alle Versuche zur Auffindung der Leichen oder des Trains vergeblich.[1]

The disaster was not soon forgotten; it was outrageous and demanded explanation. Many people, among them Fontane, attributed the tragedy to man's boldness and arrogance in defying the storming elements, as indicated in a later *Zürcherische Freitagszeitung* report of January 9, 1880: "In der Silvesternacht war nun ein furchtbarer Sturm so dass die Anwohner es für eine Vermessenheit hielten, wenn der Edinburger Zug die Passage wage."[2] Fontane, who wrote his ballad from similar newspaper accounts in the week following the accident on January 6, 1880, portrays the disaster vividly by combining realistic and supernatural elements to emphasize man's folly in a technical age. He uses the collapsed bridge to show the failure of man's attempts to dominate nature and integrates the bridge symbol into the tripartite structure of the poem to juxtapose the antagonistic elements involved.

The first stanza depicts a gathering of witches and their predictions, the second through sixth stanzas describe events in the human sphere, and the final stanza returns to the mythical landscape of the witches and the fulfillment of their prophecy. It is significant that the middle section of the ballad, representing human activities, is inserted between sections dominated by the supernatural realm. Such a framework suggests the superiority of the supernatural world. The powerlessness of the human realm in the middle section is also reflected thematically in the collapse of the bridge's "*Mittel*pfeiler."

This juxtaposition of real and supernatural worlds is

already seen in the two lines prefacing the poem, "28. Dezember 1879" and the quotation from *Macbeth*, "When shall we three meet again?" The exact date of the tragedy, designating the rational world, is contrasted with the irrational, timeless sphere of the witches. These introductory lines function to make the reader aware of the dual realms present in the ballad.

By his use of Shakespearean witches, Fontane immediately places us in a mythical world that is starkly contrasted to the real world in the middle section of the poem. Like *Macbeth*, the tragedy takes place in Scotland and concerns men who think themselves independent of higher forces outside themselves. By virtue of form and literary allusion, Fontane raises journalistic material to the status of art.

The first verse of the poem is a direct translation of the Shakespeare quotation cited: "Wann treffen wir drei wieder zusamm?" Its function is to transfer the ominous mood associated with the well-known scene from *Macbeth* to Fontane's poem. Fontane admired Shakespeare's ability to create atmosphere and utilizes the effect of the first scene for his own purposes.[3]

As in *Macbeth*, the witch's query is answered by location as well as time.

> "Um die siebente Stund, am Brückendamm."
> "Am Mittelpfeiler."

The exact hour is mentioned, in contrast to the vaguer answer given in *Macbeth*: "When the hurlyburly's done, / When the battle's lost and won." Fontane thus seeks to provide realistic detail to sustain the journalistic quality of his report. This detail is also indicated in the meeting place agreed upon by the witches: "Am Brückendamm" is narrowed even more specifically in the following verse to "Am Mittelpfeiler."

The ubiquity of the supernatural realm is suggested in the different directions from which the witches arrive:

"Ich komme vom Norden her."
"Und ich vom Süden."
"Und ich vom Meer."

Forces from various and distant regions converge on the bridge to form a focal point of future events. The anticipated disaster promises mirth and celebration for the witches: "Hei, das gibt einen Ringelreihn. . . ." The joy implied in "Ringelreihn," a metaphorical whirlwind, is in contrast to the devastation and tragedy to take place: "Und die Brücke muss in den Grund hinein." The rhyme of "Ringelreihn" and "hinein" underscores this tragic and macabre contrast.

"Ringelreihn" also characterizes the structure and tone of the first stanza. The brevity and exchange of the witches' statements create an atmosphere of excitement and expectancy. Each statement modifies and supports the other to produce a verbal "Ringelreihn." The circular pattern of dialogue formed by each witch's speaking in turn elicits a visual impression of "Ringelreihn." The frequent use of *und* to connect the statements of alternating speakers (*"Und* ich vom Süden" . . . *"Und* ich vom Meer." . . . *"Und* die Brücke . . ." . . . *"Und* der Zug") reproduces the rhythm of a roundelay. Again, the joviality inherent in the tone and rhythm of the stanza is in stark contrast to the tragic forecast of misery and suffering. Fontane is successful in writing a ballad in the original sense of the word—he creates a dance through the medium of language.

The ballad form is also supported by the frequent repetition of statements. The unanimity of the witches' decision regarding the fate of the train, for example, is echoed in the triple repetition of "muss":

". . . *muss* in den Grund hinein"
"Ei der *muss* mit."
"*Muss* mit"

"Muss" also emphasizes the inevitability of the witches' decision. The repetition of "Um die siebente Stund" in the twelfth verse again injects a realistic detail into an otherwise supernatural atmosphere.

The refrain "Tand, Tand / Ist das Gebilde von Menschen-hand" is sung by the witches in unison and underscores the dancelike rhythm of the first stanza.[4] It illustrates the omnipotence of the supernatural world over the world of men. Even before the human realm is introduced in the poem, it is declared as trifling and helpless. The actions of men portrayed in the following stanzas will thus appear pathetic in face of supernatural forces already presented.

The second stanza brings us to the setting referred to in the first stanza and introduces the human realm. Although the witches are no longer present, there is a continuity established between stanzas: the sea and directions of north and south mentioned in the first stanza are echoed in references to the water and the north and south shores in the second stanza:

> Auf der *Norderseite* das Brückenhaus—
> Alle Fenster sehen nach *Süden* aus, . . .
>   . . . ob nicht ein Licht
> *Übers Wasser* hin . . .

Unlike the first stanza, however, there is a note of anticipation and impatience now present. All windows face southward toward the bridge in expectancy of the train. The anthropomorphic description of the house as an intensive onlooker makes it the first witness of the tragedy and heightens the suspense of the stanza. The bridgekeeper and his wife also look southward at the bridge, anxiously awaiting their son:

> Und die Brückersleut ohne Rast und Ruh
> Und in Bangen sehen nach Süden zu.

The cliché "Rast und Ruh" works well to describe the typical domestic concern that the parents have for their son. The alliteration of the phrase emphasizes the restiveness of the couple. This in addition to "Bangen" describes their tenseness and contributes to the anxiety present in the atmosphere. The repetition of "sehen" as well as the "ich" of the train intensifies the mounting stress of their vigil: "alle Fenster *sehen*" . . . "und in Bangen *sehen*" . . . "*Sehen* und warten"; "Ich komme . . ." . . . "Ich komme . . ." . . . "Ich. . . ."

The style and structure of the second stanza also reflect strain and impatience. The first verse breaks off abruptly, and the resulting ellipsis creates a disturbing, alarming effect: "Auf der Norderseite, das Brückenhaus—." The ensuing repetition of *und* suggests hastiness and anxiety: "*Und* die Brücknersleut . . . / *Und* in Bangen. . . ." This repetition is also evidenced at the beginning of each stanza in the middle section:

> *Und* der Brückner jetzt: . . .
> *Und* es war der Zug . . .
> *Und* unser Stolz ist unsre Brück.

The drama of the situation is made more vivid and suspenseful by the monologue of the train. The train in the poem is not an inanimate means of transportation but, like the house with its windows, becomes an active participant in the events. Self-confidence and pride issue forth from the thrice-repeated "ich" of its statement. This repetition emphasizes the train's claim to superiority over the natural elements, and it advances despite the violence of the storm. But the train's boastful assertion becomes insignificant when compared to the dialogue in the superior realm of the witches and their repetitive "ich" statements in the first stanza of the poem ("Ich komme vom Norden her." / "Und ich vom Süden." / "Und ich vom Meer"). Stylistically the "ich . . . ich . . . ich" of the train elicits an impression of steady advance and powerful driving, the sensation of watching a steam locomotive at full speed. It is also significant that the train speaks before man as the first representative of the human realm in the poem: the technological and supernatural rather than the human and supernatural are the true antagonists in the ballad. The train is symbolic of modern technology, and man is shown in subservience to the mechanical sophistication he has created.

In the third stanza a light appears on the opposite shore in answer to the couple's anxious vigil: "Und der Brückner jetzt: 'Ich seh einen Schein / Am andern Ufer.'" The father, very much a part of the real world, is now comforted by the light that he sees. For him the train will now arrive on schedule, just as the timetable stipulates: "In elf Minuten ist er herein." His "muss" ("Das muss er sein") is in ironic contradiction to the unavoidable prediction of the witches' "muss hinein . . . muss mit . . . muss mit." Similarly, his "herein," referring to the train's safe arrival at Dundee, is in grisly contrast to the witches' "hinein," referring to the train's plunge into the depths. The speech of the old bridge-keeper is characterized by exuberance and rejoicing. There is no hesitation in his voice as his eight-verse statement describes a rosy picture of familial bliss.

The father's confidence is, however, in contrast to the mother's fear ("und in Bangen"), which has not subsided. Her apprehensive dream ("banger Traum") intuitively senses danger and no attempts by her husband will assuage her uneasiness. About what she is dreaming we are not told, but the "bange Traum" intimates the omnipresence of the supernatural and heightens the suspense. The dream strikes a somber note, but it is subordinated to the confidence that pervades the stanza.

The old man's assurance is similarly evidenced in the domestic images of the Christmas celebration:

> "Unser Johnie kommt und will seinen Baum,
> Und was noch am Baume von Lichtern ist,
> Zünd alles an wie zum heiligen Christ. . . ."

The reference to Christmas is not only intended as a contrast to the pagan world of witches. It is a sentimental image evoking middle class tranquility and comfort. The assurance that Christ and His birth provides for such a family is doubled this year ("heuer zweimal") and adds to the father's expectancy that the train will arrive. But such an expectancy proves unjustified. Although the light of the train motivates him to rekindle the candles on the Christmas tree, the mother's dark dream prevails. The father's wistful attempt to revive the Christmas spirit must remain unfulfilled, for just as Christmas is in actuality three days past, so the fate of his son is already sealed as the train hastens to its doom. The Christmas scene thus provides a dramatic contrast to the impending catastrophe. As Richard Bräutigam explains, the "Schein"—the light of the train and the light of the Christmas tree, as well as the light from the windows of the house—provides false security and equivocates the real meaning of "Schein" for the poem; all that the father sees and relies upon is only a mere *illusion* of security.[5]

In the fourth stanza the scene changes as the panting locomotive is about to enter the southern side of the bridge. The first verse confirms the bridgekeeper's sighting of the train. The antagonistic elements of storm and locomotive are emphasized with "gegen": "Am Süderturm / Keucht er vorbei jetzt *gegen* den Sturm." Now the bridgekeeper's son Johnie is introduced, who appears more audacious than his father in claiming superiority over the elements: "Die Brücke noch! / Aber was tut es, wir zwingen es doch. / . . . Wir kriegen es unter, das Element." He also has implicit confidence in the technical durability of the bridge: "Unser Stolz ist unsre Brück." "Stolz" well characterizes Johnie and his world. His hubris is that of the technocrat certain that man's scientific prowess can control the forces of nature. It is Johnie's pride—one that does not admit to the existence of superior forces—that eventually brings about his doom.

Ironically, it is just those characteristics that Johnie attributes to the storm ("Rast und ringt und rennt") that eventually conspire to defeat him. "Ringen" is reminiscent of the "Ringelreihn" whirlwind that the witches playfully anticipate in the first stanza. "Rast" (to rage) is a clever wordplay on "ohne Rast" (without rest) and thus sustains the anxious mood of the parents. "Rast und ringt und rennt" also describes the fury of the storm—all three verbs are indicative of turbulence. Their placement one after the other with the reiterated "und . . . und" creates a repetiveness suggestive of movement. Just as the "bange Traum" of the mother undermines the security of the father in the second stanza, so the relentlessness of the storm undermines Johnie's vaunted superiority and again serves to intensify the suspense. The reader is constantly reminded of the portentous forces delineated in the first stanza. In this way a structural "bridge" is created between the first and the final stanzas.

Johnie entrusts himself unquestioningly to the reliability of the locomotive and the bridge even in the midst of the storm. He emphasizes the superiority of the locomotive with its sturdy boiler and full head of steam. In contrast to the "Ich . . . ich . . . ich, der Edinburger Zug," representing the machine, Johnie assumes a collective role with "wir." He cannot function alone, for his strength is subordinated to the technological achievements of the locomotive and the bridge: "*wir* zwinge es doch," . . . "*Wir* kriegen es unter. . . ." Man's dependency is also evidenced in the parents' reliance on the bridge for their livelihood: his father is a "Brückner," the couple are "Brücknersleut" and they live in a "Brückenhaus."

Johnie's monologue is continued in the fifth stanza. His hubris continues to assert itself: "Ich lache, denk' ich an früher zurück. . . ." Johnie's pride now turns to ridicule as he scorns the old ferryboat, which hesitated to defy the elements. In the old days (implied in "früher zurück" and "alten Schifferboot") man did not have the marvels of technology to circumvent the tirades of nature, and therefore had an unpretentious respect for such forces.

Like his father's, Johnie's assurance leads him into an illusion of home and happiness, something not possible before the bridge was built:

"Wie manche Christfestnacht
Hab' ich im Fährhaus zugebracht
Und sah unsrer Fenster lichten Schein
Und zählte und konnte nicht drüben sein."

Johnie's glance is transfixed by the same "Schein" that has
assured his father and causes him to disregard the danger
of the storm. The illuminated windows in the house,
suggesting warmth and comfort, become themselves like
the light of a Christmas tree to Johnie's eyes. Again the
Christmas scene assumes a sentimental, almost melodramatic
role in view of the disaster to come. Just as Christmas is in
reality three days past, so Johnie's hopes are tragically
beyond realization as he utters his last words of arrogance.

The spotlight now once again falls on the north side of
the bridge and the house of Johnie's parents. The first four
verses of the second stanza are repeated, completing the
framework of the human realm:

Auf der Norderseite, das Brückenhaus
Alle Fenster sehen nach Süden aus,
Und die Brücknersleut ohne Rast und Ruh
Und in Bangen sehen nach Süden zu; . . .

The repetition of these lines provides more than a heighten-
ing of suspense. Their effect intensifies the anxious mood of
the second stanza to one of alarm and terror. The father no
longer admonishes his wife to abandon her "bangen Traum"
but now himself becomes fearful as the storm becomes more
furious: "Denn wütender wurde der Winde Spiel." The
alliterative w signifies the relentlessness and continued
onslaught of the storm. The witches, however, regard the
whirlwind as a joyous event ("einen Ringelreihn") and its
turbulence as playful frolic ("Spiel"). There are no bounds
or ethics in the supernatural realm—machine and man alike
are helpless playthings, dangling marionettes who only
possess the illusion of power and grandeur.

In the final scene devoted to the human domain, man's
pathetic claims to security—his locomotive and his bridge—

are struck down by a fire from heaven. A spectacular display of lightning dwarfs and negates by comparison the assuring lights of home, Christmas tree, and locomotive. The statement of one of the witches in the first stanza, "Ich lösche die Flamm . . .", now becomes clear as the lightning illuminates the waters below ("überm Wasser unten") and extinguishes the lives of the train's passengers in the watery blackness (". . . Und wieder ist Nacht"). The tenseness and suspense inherent in the preceding stanzas are now relieved with a falling rhythm paralleling the train's fall into the depths. The catharsis is complete and the witches appear satisfied in the subsequent scene.

The events of the human realm are thematically and structurally enclosed in a framework comprising the supernatural forces. Only dialogue and no narrative is contained in the first and last stanzas of the poem. The desultory, abrupt conversation and split verse structure characterizing the lightninglike quality of nature's onslaught are in contrast to the regularity of the eight-verse middle stanzas, where man's security and self-confidence are evidenced in the simple couplets and straightforward narration.

The final stanza returns to the supernatural realm. The witches have witnessed the destruction of man and machine and rejoice in having attained their goal. The first verse of the poem is repeated and, like a leitmotif, reinvokes the eerie atmosphere of the first stanza. In contrast to the introduction, however, the time and place agreed upon no longer describe a specific setting. Midnight, the traditional bewitching hour, as well as the high location, "Bergeskamm . . . hohen Moor . . . Erlenstamm," emphasize the transcendent and nebulous mythical realm. The three crones now happily anticipate providing an account of the "Zahl," "Namen" and "Qual" of their victims as their "Hei!" reiterates the jubilance of the first stanza. The count of bodies ("Zahl") appears as a macabre contrast to Johnie's sentimental count of the lighted windows in the previous stanza ("und *zählte* und konnte nicht drüben sein."). "Qual" ironically reflects the "Jammer und Not" that Johnie had presumptuously thought to escape on this trip. The witches prove their absolute sovereignty with their ability to identify the names of each victim while they themselves remain anonymous, disembodied voices. The witches rejoice over the destruction of the bridge: "Wie Splitter brach das Gebälk entzwei." One can hear the collapsing girders in the sound of "Splitter." "Entzwei" indicates a fragmentation of the human sphere of comfort and appears as a tragic antithesis to the father's desire to celebrate Christmas "heuer zweimal." The final chorus now repeats the playful chant of the first stanza, as man's attempts to defy nature appear trifling: "Tand, Tand / Ist das Gebilde von Menschenhand."

In the first and last stanzas Fontane establishes a poetic landscape of myth, which constitutes a removal from the reality of the disaster. The borrowed Shakespeare quotation is immediate evidence of this artistic transcendence over the events depicted in the middle section of the poem. The aesthetic distance achieved distinguishes the poem as a "Kunstballade"—the facts having been filtered through the poet's artistic sense and given new form and significance. In this way Fontane uses the event to express something far more profound than a journalistic account could relate.

Also, in the middle section Fontane stylistically maintains poetic distance in an effort to avoid the brutality of the situation. The accident is not depicted directly from Johnie's perspective, but rather is viewed indirectly from the shore. We hear the fury of the elements and see the splendor of the "Feuer vom Himmel" rather than the destruction of train and bridge. Fontane is more intent on a poetic than a realistic or naturalistic effect, as Fritz Martini comments: "Das eigentliche Geschehen kommt ja nicht auf den faktischen Vorgang, sondern auf seine inneren und gefühlhaften Bedeutungen."[6] The selective, aesthetic eye of the artist is continually at work—we see snapshots of action rather than the whole event. It is this aesthetic eye, accompanied by the poet's insight, that gives the event its significance.

Related to the poet's artistic control is his use of the

bridge as the principle symbolic, thematic, and structural component of the poem. Symbolically, the bridge represents the intersection of reality and myth and indicates Fontane's ability to depict the catastrophic moment of confrontation between the two. Thematically, the bridge epitomizes technical achievement in the modern age. It forms an image of man's superiority over nature, a superiority that is only illusory and must inevitably crumble in face of greater powers. Ultimately then, there is no bridge between man and the forces holding him in abeyance, for these forces are irrevocably in control. Structurally, the bridge is visualized in the mid-section of the poem, which spans the abyss between the first and final stanzas. While man's physical bridge falls asunder, an artistic "bridge," comprising the dark motif of the mother's dream and supernatural forces behind the storm, joins the introduction and conclusion of the poem. Fontane's final achievement is found in his integration of the multiple aspects of the bridge metaphor, which provide the poem with artistic unity. The poet thus assumes the elevated role of creator and destroyer in playing with man's foibles and illustrating their subordination to the forces of art and myth.

7

Friedrich Nietzsche : "Venedig"

Venedig

An der Brücke stand
jüngst ich in brauner Nacht.
Fernher kam Gesang:
goldener Tropfen quoll's
über die zitternde Fläche weg.
Gondeln, Lichter, Musik—
trunken schwamm's in die Dämmrung hinaus . . .

Meine Seele, ein Saitenspiel,
sang sich, unsichtbar berührt,
heimlich ein Gondellied dazu,
zitternd vor bunter Seligkeit.
—Hörte jemand ihr zu? . . .

Friedrich Nietzsche wrote "Venedig" in the fall of 1888, shortly before the mental collapse from which he never recovered. Nietzsche's style, vigor, and poetic vision reach their zenith in the works written in this last year of his productive life. In the preface to his autobiography, *Ecce Homo*, in which "Venedig" appears, Nietzsche writes:

> An diesem vollkommnen Tage, wo alles reift und nicht
> nur die Traube braun wird, fiel mir eben ein Sonnenblick
> auf mein Leben: ich sah rückwärts, ich sah hinaus
> ich sah nie so viel und so gute Dinge auf einmal.[1]

Yet, in this aura of harmony and well-being Nietzsche was never able to discount his fear and loneliness. As he also states in *Ecce Homo*, "Ich weiss das Glück, nicht ohne Schauder von Furchtsamkeit zu denken."[2] Such contradictory elements of harmony and alienation pervade "Venedig."

The poem represents Nietzsche's attempt to assimilate the objective phenomena perceived by his senses in order to bring the outwardly observed beauty within himself. Such internalization is illustrated in the first stanza with the images of "brauner Nacht" and "goldener Tropfen." In the second stanza the assimilative process is augmented and embraces the innermost recesses of the poet's soul: "Meine Seele, ein Saitenspiel, / sang sich, unsichtbar berührt. . . ." The final achievement of the poem is more than a mere aesthetic appreciation of the Venetian scene, for it assumes deeper connotations of a spiritual nature with the words "heimlich . . . unsichtbar . . . berührt . . . Seele . . . Seligkeit." The poem represents an intensely personal experience combining the internal spiritual realm of the poet with the objective outer world. Yet in the last verse this harmony is shattered by the fear of loneliness—the "Schauder von Furchtsamkeit" mentioned earlier. The poet cannot perpetuate this perfected moment and realizes his essential isolation: "Hörte jemand ihr zu? . . . ." For Nietzsche, the shock of alienation must inevitably follow successful communion with the objective world and his poem must question the harmonious interchange of elements perceived.

The first stanza of the poem embraces Nietzsche's physical situation. He is standing at the bridge, at the symbolic threshold of transition, and his senses respond to visual and aural stimuli surrounding him. The reader is able to view a spatial relation of sights and sounds to the poet: "*Fernher* kam Gesang: . . ," "goldener Tropfen quoll's . . . weg," "trunken schwamm's in die Dämmerung *hinaus*." Although impressionistic images ("braune Nacht," "goldene Tropfen") are already present in the first stanza, the scene itself is not yet completely assimilated by the poet. The transference from the physical to the spiritual self occurs principally in the second stanza, where we are no longer aware of distance and direction. The outer scene has been transmuted to an inner landscape, which is "unsichtbar" and "heimlich." The poet speaks now of his soul as a lyre, which plays in harmony with the outward beauty he observes:

> Meine Seele, ein Saitenspiel,
> sang sich, unsichtbar berührt,
> heimlich ein Gondellied dazu. . . .

Although the images of the first stanza do not have the same degree of internalization as the second, the nature of the images evoked points toward the final harmony achieved. The initial image encountered, that of the bridge, is the first and most significant of these. The bridge designates transition and communication between otherwise separated areas and thus reflects precisely the poet's own condition—he must "bridge" the interstice between his innermost soul and the stimuli of the outer world. The fact that the poet is standing motionless at the bridge is also significant. He is figuratively placed between two realms that present opposing alternatives. His position between these alternatives creates a tension expressed twice in the poem with "zitternd": "goldener Tropfen quoll's / über die *zitternde* Fläche weg" and "Meine Seele, ein Saitenspiel, sang sich . . . *zitternd* vor bunter Seligkeit." Physical movement in one direction or another would destroy the delicate balance and harmony the poet seeks to achieve.

The second image of "brauner Nacht" likewise emphasizes the coalescence of external and internal realms. It unifies the opposites of day and night and thereby achieves a momentary suspension of time. "Braune Nacht" and, later, "Dämmerung" signify a transitionary and evanescent moment when light and darkness appear combined. This moment belongs to both realms and yet is discretely independent of each. The harmony between daylight and darkness evokes a natural image that parallels the private harmony established by the poet between inner and outer worlds. The approaching darkness also anticipates the end of this harmony of light and flow of golden droplets in the final verse.

Like the images of the bridge and the brown night, the "Gesang" combined with "Gondeln, Lichter, Musik" in the first stanza, also anticipates the final harmony achieved by the poet. The music is not only moving toward the poet ("Fernher kam Gesang . . .") but together with the gondolas and lights flows outward to pervade the evening scene ("trunken schwamm's in die Dämmrung hinaus . . ."). Thus a balance is achieved in the juxtaposition of "fernher" and "hinaus," which refers to the passage of music toward and away from the listener. The two words suggest the two realms represented in the poem—that which approaches and becomes part of the poet ("fernher"), and that which pervades the outer scene ("hinaus"). "Fernher" also suggests the isolation of the poet—until this moment he has been divorced from the outer stimuli that now enrich him inwardly. The music allows him to abandon his isolation and harmonize with the outer world. A "bridge" of communication is thus established.

Nietzsche also integrates this music into the sounds of his poem. He uses synesthesia to create a union of normally separated spheres. "Goldene Tropfen," describing the song, combines aural and visual stimuli: the richness of the *o* sounds produces a "golden" tone enabling the reader to "see" the sounds and "hear" the color. Again the initial image of the bridge is evoked in the poet's synthesis of these normally separate realms of color and sound.

The delicate balance achieved in the images of "braune Nacht" and "goldene Tropfen," together with the static verb "stand," produces a moment of tension. Nietzsche's poem has seized this moment and made it stand still in time. The moment might be pictured as a ballet dancer poised on one toe, standing still, yet imperceptibly quivering ("zitternd") due to the precariousness of his or her position.

The final two verses of the stanza support and expand the preceding images:

> goldener Tropfen quoll's
> über die zitternde Fläche weg.
> Gondeln, Lichter, Musik—
> trunken schwamm's in die Dämmrung hinaus . . .

Again we are presented with an amalgam of visual and aural realms in the words "Gondeln, Lichter, Musik." The poet treats these as aggregated elements flowing into the sunset. "Trunken" suggests the poet's intoxicated condition: his senses are fully occupied in a brief moment of elation when he is able to figuratively immerse himself in the combination of colors and sounds surrounding him. "Quellen" and "schwamm's" are synonymous in suggesting the liquid motion with which the various elements flow together to produce the poet's euphoria. This liquid motion is reflected in the liquid sounds of "goldener" and "Quellen." The "braune Nacht" mentioned in the second verse is now again alluded to with the word "Dämmerung," a moment when objects and colors are no longer distinct but appear to merge harmoniously (the Impressionist Claude Monet, for example, uses the sunset to achieve this illusion of harmony). "Trunken" implies the poet's total submersion in the harmony of sounds and colors, yet simultaneously anticipates the final dissolution of this harmony. It indicates an inherent instability which ultimately rends the perfected moment and leaves the poet in isolation. "Trunken" characterizes an ecstatic Dionysian moment that engenders its own destruction. The intoxication of poetic expression, as Nietzsche implies in *Zarathustra,* is fragile because it must remain incomprehensible to anyone outside the poet's perception: "Was bin ich? Eine trunkene süsse Leier,—eine Mitternachts-

Leier, eine Glocken-Unke, die Niemand versteht, aber welche reden *muss,* vor Tauben, . . . Denn ihr versteht mich nicht!"[3]

The three points of suspension after the final word, "hinaus," suggest the infinite journey of the color and music into the evening sunset. The picture of the outer scene thus becomes progressively larger and more universal as the poet's introspection becomes deeper and more in touch with his inner self. The three periods function also as a pause and a final transition from the poet's outer to his inner self. The *s* sound of the last verse ("*schwamm's hinaus*") is retained in the first two lines of the second stanza ("Seele, Saiten*s*piel, *s*ang *s*ich, un*s*ichtbar"), forming an alliterative "bridge" between external and internal realms.

With the second stanza the Venetian landscape becomes totally assimilated. The words and images used allude to those of the first stanza, but now they concern the poet's soul rather than his physical situation. The aspects of color and light are preserved but become intangible and muted privately within the poet's spirit. The song is still present ("Meine Seele, ein Saitenspiel, sang sich . . . ein Gondellied dazu . . .") but now becomes personally secluded ("heim-lich") and inwardly contained ("sang *sich*"). The color of the scene remains ("bunte Seligkeit") but is now veiled ("unsichtbar") within the poet's intuition. The tension char-acterizing the outer scene ("goldener Tropfen quoll's / über die *zitternde* Fläche weg.") parallels the potential within the poet's soul ("Meine Seele . . .sang sich . . .*zitternd* vor bunter Seligkeit."). The image of the gondola is carried from the first stanza ("*Gondeln,* Lichter, Musik") but is now com-bined with "Lied" ("ein Gondellied"), forming a word that synthesizes the two media of sight and sound. Nietzsche uses the lyre ("Saitenspiel") as an instrument that attunes the poet's soul to the beauty of the outer scene ("Meine Seele sang sich . . . ein Gondellied *dazu*"). Thus, like the bridge, the lyre brings the two realms into harmony and communion.

The inner sphere of private experience in the second stanza represents to the poet more than a mere aesthetic appreciation, however. The intoxication of this moment becomes a spiritual experience, which for Nietzsche approaches a mystical vision. Like the mystic, Nietzsche seeks to verbalize his innermost spiritual sensations through meditation. The vocabulary he employs is close to that of the mystics and pietists. His usage of the word "berührt," for example, to describe the communion of his soul with the outward scene, is evidenced frequently in mystical and pietistic writings. August Langen includes "berühren" in his *Wortschatz des Pietismus*: "In der Mystik ist der Terminus gebräuchlich; wahrscheinlich wurde er aus ihr in die religiösen Strömungen der folgenden Jahrhunderte über-nommen und in unmittelbarer Überlieferung dem Pietismus zugeleitet."[4] The words "heimlich" and "unsichtbar" sim-ilarly denote the intuitive, mystical nature of the poet's experience. Yet Nietzsche is not mystical in the traditional sense, for his communion is not with God, but with the beauty that surrounds him. He finds that which is divine in the realm of art.

The final harmony achieved within the poem is also reflected in the innate musical qualities of each verse.[5] Nietzsche was continually preoccupied with music in his own essays (e.g., *Die Geburt der Tragödie aus dem Geiste der Musik*), and he found in the city of Venice the epitome of his musical endeavor: "Wenn ich ein anderes Wort für Musik suche, so finde ich nur das Wort Venedig."[6] The poem thus becomes a lyrical mixture of words and sounds. As in "Venedig," Nietzsche also has Zarathustra express this relationship between words and music with the bridge image:

Wie lieblich ist es, dass Worte und Töne da sind: sind nicht Worte und Töne Regenbogen und Schein-Brücken zwischen Ewig-Geschiedenem? Zu jeder Seele gehört eine andere Welt; für jede Seele ist jede andre Seele eine Hinterwelt. Zwischen dem Ähnlichsten gerade lügt der Schein am schönsten; denn die kleinste Kluft ist am schwersten zu überbrücken. Für mich—wie gäbe es ein Ausser-mir? Es giebt kein Aussen! Aber das vergessen wir bei allen Tönen; wie lieblich ist es,

dass wir vergessen! Sind nicht den Dingen Namen und Töne
geschenkt, dass der Mensch sich an den Dingen erquicke? . . .
Wie lieblich ist alles Reden und alle Lüge der Töne! Mit
Tönen tanzt unsre Liebe auf bunten Regenbögen.[7]

"Venedig" represents a musical composition in words.
The alliterative and assonantal qualities of the poem produce
the most salient musical characteristics ("Brücke-brauner,
goldener Tropfen quoll's, Seele-Saitenspiel-sang sich-
unsichtbar-Seligkeit"). Words of music and song are frequent
throughout the poem ("Gesang . . . Musik . . . Saitenspiel . . .
sang sich . . . Gondellied") and implement the harmonious
exchange between exterior and interior realms. The combination of vowels and liquids produces long sounds that
describe the flow of golden droplets into the distance
("goldener Tropfen quoll's"). The liquid sounds are echoed
in the second stanza ("Seele, Saitenspiel, heimlich, Gondellied"), thus forming a tonal "bridge" between outer and
inner realms. The inherent musical qualities of the poem are
supported by the evidence that Nietzsche actually *sang*
"Venedig" shortly after the onset of his madness while
traveling from Turin, Italy, to Basel, Switzerland.[8] Unfortunately the melody is lost, for no one recorded it. But the
incident does suffice to emphasize that music and words
were intimately associated for Nietzsche, especially in this
poem.

The aural richness of "Venedig" combines with the visual
imagery of color and light to attain a shimmering ecstasy
of the soul. The poet must draw on all stimuli of the senses
to find solace from his isolation. He embraces the universe
by literally reverberating ("Zitternd") with its sounds and
colors. The achievement of the poet is found in that evanescent moment when the boundaries between the solitary
poet and the outer world are obliterated and both become
united in harmony. But unfortunately such union can exist
for only a moment. The simultaneous instability of ecstasy,
anticipated with "trunken," irrevocably destroys the perfected balance and leaves the poet once again aware of his
isolation: "—Hörte jemand ihr zu? . . ." The dash serves

to separate the stream of consciousness built up in the former verses. The flow of images is suddenly severed as the poet is jarred from his reverie. His perfunctory, final question forms a stark contrast to the sustained *s* alliteration and extended reflection of the preceding six-verse sentence. Nietzsche thus creates an idyllic moment only to destroy it in the end.[9] As stated above, he cannot conceive of pleasure without pain, and thus in the poem he acknowledges the fundamental ambivalence of perception inherent in the creative process. The last line poses a final question that will find no answer. As Johannes Klein remarks, " 'Venedig' ist ein fragendes Gedicht, eine fragwürdige Welt, wenn auch eine schöne Welt."[10]

The perfected moment of euphoria and intoxication found in this poem is also delineated by Nietzsche in his doctrine of Eternal Recurrence. It engenders a momentary suspension of time when the poet experiences life in its highest intensity, yet life that is totally silent and still. A passage reflecting the imagery of "Venedig" is found in the section "At Noontide" of *Zarathustra*:

Oh Glück! Oh Glück! Willst du wohl singen, oh meine Seele? Du liegst im Grase. Aber das ist die heimliche feierliche Stunde, wo kein Hirt seine Flöte bläst. Scheue dich! Heisser Mittag schläft auf den Fluren. Singe nicht! Still! Die Welt ist vollkommen.[11]

As in "Venedig," however, the bliss of such a moment must pass as Zarathustra awakes once again. He too must question the beauty he has experienced and ask if the song of his soul has been heard:

Auf! sprach er zu sich selber, du Schläfer! . . . Oh Himmel über mir, sprach er seufzend und setzte sich aufrecht, du schaust mir zu? Du horchst meiner wunderlichen Seele zu? . . . Wann trinkst du meine Seele in dich zurück? Also sprach Zarathustra und erhob sich von seinem Lager am Baume wie aus einer fremden Trunkenheit.[12]

Another such moment is found in Nietzsche's depiction of Pan at noon in *Der Wanderer und sein Schatten*:

Wem ein tätiger und sturmreicher Morgen des Lebens beschieden war, dessen Seele überfällt um den Mittag des Lebens eine seltsame Ruhesucht, die Monden und Jahre lang dauern kann. Es wird still um ihn, die Stimmen klingen fern und ferner; die Sonne scheint steil auf ihn herab. Auf einer verborgenen Waldwiese sieht er den grossen Pan schlafend; alle Dinge der Natur sind mit ihm eingeschlafen, einen Ausdruck von Ewigkeit im Gesichte—so dünkt es ihm. Er will nichts, er sorgt sich um nichts, sein Herz steht still, nur sein Auge lebt—es ist ein Tod mit wachen Augen. Vieles sieht da der Mensch, was er nie sah, und soweit er sieht, ist Alles in ein Lichtnetz eingesponnen und gleichsam darin begraben. Er fühlt sich glücklich dabei, aber es ist ein schweres, schweres Glück.— Da endlich erhebt sich der Wind in den Bäumen, Mittag ist vorbei, das *Leben* reisst ihn wieder an sich, das Leben mit blinden Augen, hinter dem sein Gefolge herstürmt: Wunsch, Trug, Vergessen, Geniessen, Vernichten, Vergänglichkeit. Und so kommt der Abend herauf, stürmreicher und tatenvoller, als selbst der Morgen war. — Den eigentlich tätigen Menschen erscheinen die länger währenden Zustände des Erkennens fast unheimlich und krankhaft; aber nicht unangenehm.[13]

The characteristic ambivalence of this passage ("ein Tod mit wachen Augen . . . Alles in ein Lichtnetz eingesponnen und gleichsam darin begraben . . . ein schweres, schweres Glück . . . fast unheimlich und krankhaft; aber nicht unangenehm") is also evidenced in "Venedig." Nietzsche ultimately distrusts the validity of poetic expression. The poem must end in query, because Nietzsche is unable to convince himself of the perfection of language that poetry entails. Language, however beautiful, must ultimately prove a lie. As he says in one of his *Dionysos-Dithyramben*:

Nein, nur ein Dichter!
ein Tier
das lügen muss,
das wesentlich, willentlich lügen muss.[14]

In "Venedig" the poet must therefore experience the loneliness that inevitably accompanies momentary harmony. In the end he must call his own creation into question, because only the poet's words—never the poet—are able to cross the symbolic bridge to final perfection. The poem from the *Dionysos-Dithyramben* continues:

> Nur Narr! Nur Dichter!
> . . . herumsteigend auf lügnerischen *Wortbrücken,*
> auf Lügen-Regenbogen
> zwischen falschen Himmeln
> Herumschweifend, herumschleichend
> nur Narr, nur Dichter. (italics added)

It is significant that the poet stands motionless at the bridge. Although his reflections achieve transitory fulfillment, the physical stasis of the first verse anticipates the paralysis of the final question. The other side of the bridge must remain a potential. Yet, according to Nietzsche, it is this ultimate inability to sustain perfection that provides man with a measure of greatness. His fundamental ambivalence renders him unable to complete passage of the bridge, yet he does achieve a momentary intimation of reaching the other side. As Nietzsche writes in *Zarathustra*, "Was gross ist am Menschen, das ist, dass er eine Brücke und kein Zweck ist."[15]

8

Rainer Maria Rilke :
"Pont du Carrousel"

Pont du Carrousel

Der blinde Mann, der auf der Brücke steht,
grau wie ein Markstein namenloser Reiche,
er ist vielleicht das Ding, das immer gleiche,
um das von fern die Sternenstunde geht,
und der Gestirne stiller Mittelpunkt.
Denn alles um ihn irrt und rinnt und prunkt.

Er ist der unbewegliche Gerechte,
in viele wirre Wege hingestellt;
der dunkle Eingang in die Unterwelt
bei einem oberflächlichen Geschlechte.

Die spanische Landschaft, Toledo, hat meine Verfassung zum
Äussersten getrieben: indem dort, das äussere Ding selbst:
Turm, Berg, Brücke zugleich schon die unerhörte, unüber-
treffliche Intensität der inneren Äquivalente besass, durch
die man es hätte darstellen mögen. Erscheinung und Vision

kamen gleichsam überall im Gegenstand zusammen, es war
in jedem eine ganze Innenwelt herausgestellt, als ob ein
Engel, der den Raum umfasst, blind wäre und in sich
schaute. Diese, nicht mehr von Menschen aus, sondern im
Engel geschaute Welt, ist vielleicht meine wirkliche Aufgabe,
wenigstens kämen in ihr alle meine früheren Versuche
zusammen.[1]

Although Rilke's "Pont du Carrousel" was inspired by
a French rather than a Spanish scene, it nevertheless
illustrates the substance of the above quotation. The world
of tangible objects—here the tower, the mountain, and
the bridge—possesses an intangible inner essence, which
the poet aspires to comprehend and describe. "Pont du
Carrousel," written by Rilke in Paris in 1902, was included in a volume of poems entitled *Das Buch der Bilder*.
It is typical of Rilke's "Dinggedichte," in which the poet
seeks to discover the inner essence of each "thing" and
reveal its symbolic significance: "Jedes Ding ist ein Raum,
eine Möglichkeit, und an mir liegt es, diese vollkommen
oder mangelhaft poetisch zu erfüllen."[2] The angel of the
above quotation, whose blindness enables greater introspection, has his counterpart in the blind man of the poem. The
bridge on which he stands acquires the "unerhörte, unüber-
treffliche Intensität" of the bridge in Toledo in its symbolic
ability to connect the outer and inner realms of existence.

The poem centers around the figure of the blind man
standing on a bridge. The initial images identify him as the
temporal and spatial center point of existence: he is "das
immer gleiche," "der Gestirne stiller Mittelpunkt" as well
as "der unbewegliche Gerechte." The blind man probes an
inner world of thought and feeling not seen by those dis-
tracted by the visible realm.[3] The import of this figure is not
immediately apparent, but becomes clearer as the poem
progresses: it expresses his significance as a physical representative of the central, inner world of the spirit, around
which all else revolves.

The blind man is "grau wie ein Markstein namenloser
Reiche." "Markstein" is a metaphor that emphasizes the

man's ability to define that which is otherwise vague or indistinct. Although the realms surrounding him are "namenlos," he can provide boundaries and identity. He is the only distinct point in an anonymous context. "Markstein" is the only tangible object in an otherwise nameless world. As a boundary stone, the blind man represents a transition between realms. His intermediary condition is also seen in his position on the bridge. Like the stone, he is not part of the lands that he divides, but provides a connecting point. "Grau" also connotes this intermediary standpoint as the tonal transition between black and white. This depiction of the blind man as a center is consistent throughout the poem.

The solitary condition of the man is also suggested in the first two verses. He stands as an isolated figure on the bridge—there is no one or nothing accompanying him. "Grau" and "Stein" connote a colorless, almost inorganic condition. He is not part of the realms for which he provides boundaries but is assigned to a remote border position. In this aloof situation all seems distant and "namenlos." But Rilke does not view such isolation negatively. It is a necessary condition if each "thing" is to be revealed in its essence, "denn die Dinge geben sich ganz nur, wenn sie in die bereiten zärtlichen Hände eines Einsamen geraten."[4] Solitude offers Rilke communion with the center of existence and removes him from that which is superfluous or nonessential: "Vielleicht kommt dort die Einsamkeit über mich und die grosse Stille, nach der alles in mir verlangt; dann will ich still leben im Umgang mit Dingen und dankbar sein für alles, was Alltägliches abhält von mir. . . . Meine Einsamkeit schliesst sich endlich, und ich bin in der Arbeit wie der Kern in der Frucht. . . ."[5] The "Kern in der Frucht" expresses the same centrality and essence as those of the blind man in "Pont du Carrousel."[6]

Subsequent verses describe the blind man as the possible ("vielleicht") temporal as well as spatial midpoint of the universe:

> Er ist vielleicht das Ding, das immer gleiche,
> um das von fern die Sternenstunde geht,
> und der Gestirne stiller Mittelpunkt.

In referring to the blind man as "das Ding," Rilke raises him to symbolic value consistent with the poet's "Dinggedicht." For Rilke, the "Ding" is the outer form which is possessed with a unique inner identity. Each of his "Dinggedichte" attempts to capture this inner identity to accomplish his task. Thus the poet's hesitancy in identifying his poetic treatment of the man is expressed in the uncertainty of "vielleicht." This does not undermine the stature of the man, however, who acquires transcendent value as a "Ding" symbol. The blind man is a manifestation of that central essence which Rilke seeks to know in all things:

> In jedem Ding will ich eine Nacht ruhen, wenn ich am Tage mit meinem Tun durch die anderen Dinge ging. — Bei jedem Ding will ich einmal schlafen, von seiner Wärme müd werden, auf seinen Atemzügen auf und nieder träumen, seine liebe gelöste nackte Nachbarschaft an allen meinen Gliedern spüren und stark werden durch den Duft seines Schlafes und dann am Morgen früh, eh es erwacht, vor allem Abschied, weitergehen, weitergehen.[7]

The poet himself is like the blind man, the "Ding" physically personifying the inner core of existence; he says in "Die spanische Trilogie," for example, "aus mir und alledem ein einzig Ding zu machen, Herr."[8] This "Ding" does not change with time but remains always the same ("das immer gleiche um das von fern die Sternenstunde geht . . ."). The vastness of the outer world, already referred to in the second verse ("namenloser Reiche"), takes on cosmic proportions with "Sternenstunde," the sidereal hour based on the motion of the stars. Whereas time passes in the revolving outer universe, the blind man remains constant and is therefore able to transcend time. "Sternenstunde" also implies an ordered, harmonious universe of which the blind man is the center. The word is related to "Sternstunde," which means a propitious hour of fulfillment and triumph. "Geht" refers to the movement of the stars in direct contrast to "steht" which indicates the stationary position of the blind man, and "von fern" emphasizes his central and pivotal position. Through each "Ding," Rilke seeks to overcome the transience of life by viewing it in essential qualities: "Das Ding ist bestimmt . . . von allem Zufall fortgenommen, jeder Unklarheit entrückt, der Zeit enthoben und dem Raum gegeben, ist es dauernd geworden, fähig zur Ewigkeit."[9] "Der Gestirne stiller Mittelpunkt" is consistent with "Sternenstunde" in its reference to the stars, but emphasizes the blind man's spatial centrality rather than temporal transcendence.

The final verse of the first stanza, "Denn alles um ihn irrt und rinnt und prunkt," introduces the confused activity surrounding the blind man as we are provided with a contrast to the preceding harmony of the outer "Ding" symbol and its inner essence. "Sternenstunde," suggesting order and regularity, is now replaced by a different activity that also surrounds the blind man, but the verbs imply universal ("alles") disorder and confusion. This last verse thus disturbs the cosmos implied in "Sternenstunde" and establishes a dichotomy between the blind man as the "stiller Mittelpunkt" and the frenzied world about him. The chaos of this outer world is reflected in the syntax as well as in the verbal meanings. "Denn alles um ihn irrt und rinnt und prunkt" is not a complete sentence but a fragment dependent for its meaning on the preceding lines. The triple verb repetition emphasizes the motion of the external world in contrast to the motionless inner realm ("stiller Mittelpunkt"). This motion is not only implied in the meaning of the verbs; their placement after one another with "und . . . und" creates a tempo suggestive of movement. Yet there is no progression or specific order indicated in the verbal placement—there is no rationale or direction toward anything. This disorder, indicated with "irrt" and enforced by the quickness of "rinnt," is contrary to "geht," which characterizes the regularity of "Sternenstunde." "Prunkt," suggesting superficiality and ostentation, is contrasted with the rhyming

"Mittelpunkt," which characterizes the essential qualities of the blind man.

There is thus a duality established in the first stanza between stillness and motion, between inner and outer worlds, between cosmos and chaos. The bridge becomes on one hand symbolic of the link between the physical figure of the man and his metaphysical essence and also a metaphor for the passage from superficiality and confusion to permanence and durability. Rilke uses the bridge symbol in a similar manner in an unpublished letter of 1914: "Die Brücke führt hinüber zur Seite der Beständigkeit, die dem Wankelmut des Menschen gegenübergestellt wird."[10] Rilke contrasts the "Ding," the object that he strives to comprehend poetically, with the confused, superficial world: "Alle Dinge sind so bereit, unsere vielen und oft verirrten Gedanken und Wünsche zu bewirten, für kleine Zeit. . . . Denn da Menschen und Verhältnisse eigenmächtig sind und sich ewig verwirren, woran soll man sich messen dürfen, wenn nicht an den willigen Dingen?"[11] The blind man's position *on* the bridge and not to either side is thus indicative of his intermediary position between dichotomous extremes.

The second stanza provides further illustration of the thoughts presented in the first stanza. It continues to describe the blind man as the only stability in the confusion of the external world:

> Er ist der unbewegliche Gerechte,
> in viele wirre Wege hingestellt;
> der dunkle Eingang in die Unterwelt
> bei einem oberflächlichen Geschlechte.

"Unbeweglich" is reminiscent of "steht" and "*stiller* Mittelpunkt" of the first stanza. For Rilke, stillness is a virtue that abides only in the "Dingen": "Eine Stille ist um die Dinge. Alle Bewegung legt sich, wird Kontur, und aus vergangener und künftiger Zeit schliesst sich ein Dauerndes: der Raum, die grosse Beruhigung der zu nichts gedrängten Dinge."[12] Rilke frequently emphasized the stillness and isolation he needed as poet: "Meine Arbeit war immer so sehr vom Alleinsein inspiriert, dass ich rein positiv, nicht aus Menschenscheu, um ihretwillen die Stille wünschen muss, besonders, wo so viel Hemmnis und Schrecken innerlich gutzumachen bleibt."[13]

"Gerechte" suggests the order and universal law that Rilke also associated with the "Ding" and that he uses as an additional characterization of the blind man ("der unbewegliche Gerechte"): "Die Dinge sind untrüglich! Sie enthalten am reinsten die Gesetze."[14] The harmony found in this law is associated with the harmony found in "Sternenstunde." To discover the beauty of an object is to discover its conformity to law "Die Dinge sind vollkommen, sie stellen das Gesetz dar und die Gesetzmässigkeit, die dauern. . . ."[15] The second verse, "in viele wirre Wege hingestellt," once again contrasts this inner realm of harmony with the outside world of "irren," "rinnen," and "prunken."

The final two verses continue the description of the blind man's function:

> Er ist . . .
> der dunkle Eingang in die Unterwelt
> bei einem oberflächlichen Geschlechte.

His position on the bridge also places him at the threshold of the underworld. This "Unterwelt" is not to be interpreted as a negative realm, but one that exists under the turbulent superficial world to symbolize spiritual depth and essence. This lower realm is frequently an allusion to death in Rilke's poetry. The inward turn of the dead person's eyes provides an inner clarity in the *Neue Gedichte,* for example. "Dunkle" characterizes this subterranean world by opposing it to the visible outer realm of the stars. "Dunkle" also corresponds to the darkness of the man's blindness, and Rilke relates this darkness to the origin and essence of being:

> Du Dunkelheit, aus der ich stamme,
> ich liebe dich mehr als die Flamme.[16]

Just as blindness suggests introspection, darkness implies depth of perception and being:

> Ich liebe meines Wesens Dunkelstunden
> in welchen meine Sinne sich vertiefen.[17]

Much as the blind man is timeless ("das immer gleiche") as the center point of the universe, Rilke conceives of night and darkness as representative of eternity:

> Ich ertrug, vom befangenen Körper aus,
> Nächte, ja, ich befreundete
> ihn, den irdenen, mir der Unendlichkeit.[18]

The "Unterwelt" is achieved by a descent ("Abstieg") into the loneliness and quietude of the self:

> Die Einsamkeit wird sich erweitern und wird eine dämmernde Wohnung werden, daran der Lärm der andern fern vorübergeht . . . Der Abstieg in Ihr Einsames wird eine Einkehr, die zu eigenen, guten, reichen und weiten Wegen führen mögen.[19]

"Oberflächlichen Geschlechte" restates the superficiality found previously in "prunken." It is in direct contrast to "der unbewegliche Gerechte": assonance and alliteration provide a similarity of sound ("unbewegliche" and "oberflächliche" are also the only five-syllable words in the poem), yet opposite realms are depicted. "Geschlechte," however, is the first word that specifically implicates the world of men as a part of that which "irrt und rinnt und prunkt," and is separate from the world of "Dinge," which has spiritual identity and universal order. Rilke must be free of this world of men so as to ponder the true identity of the blind man: "Nur lebt man oft . . . völlig in der Welt der Dinge, wo Menschen nicht vorkommen, . . . als wäre man der einzige Mensch."[20] Simenauer comments on Rilke's opposing worlds of men and "Dinge":

Es gibt kaum eine Stelle von den Dingen bei Rilke, wo er sie nicht dem Menschen gegenüberstellt; der Mensch wird dabei immer zu leicht befunden: er ist unzulänglich, immer willkürlich, er verwirrt sich ewig, ist zu eigenmächtig und vergänglich. Menschen können ihm nicht helfen, er ist von ihnen durch einen Zwischenraum getrennt.[21]

The title of the poem is significant in that the bridge offers an alternative to the hectic outer world. The carrousel of life offers no direction but travels only in endless circles of distraction. The bridge provides a path to the inner realm of the spirit. The only outer correspondence to this inner realm is the blind man, who at the center of the carrousel offers definition ("Markstein") in the anonymity ("namenlos") of confusion.

This quest for inner identity demonstrates Rilke's similarity to the romantic poets. Like Rilke, Novalis sought to disregard the outer world and attain the inner spirit:

Wir träumen von Reisen durch das Weltall: ist denn das Weltall nicht in uns? Die Tiefen unseres Geistes kennen wir nicht.—Nach Innen geht der geheimnisvolle Weg. In uns, oder nirgends ist die Ewigkeit mit ihren Welten, die Vergangenheit und Zukunft. Die Aussenwelt ist die Schattenwelt, sie wirft ihren Schatten in das Lichtreich. Jetzt scheint es uns freilich innerlich so dunkel, einsam gestaltlos, aber wie ganz anders wird es uns dünken, wenn diese Verfinsterung vorbei, und der Schattenkörper hinweggerückt ist. Wir werden mehr geniessen als je, denn unser Geist hat entbehrt. . . . Die innere Welt ist gleichsam mehr mein als die äussre. Sie ist so innig, so heimlich. Man möchte ganz in ihr leben.[22]

In a vein similar to that of Novalis, Rilke remarks in his Seventh Elegy: "Nirgends wird Welt sein, als innen,"[23] and an earlier poem, "Die Insel," emphasizes this inner realm: "Nah ist nur Innres; alles andre fern."[24] Rilke's symbolic use of the bridge as a connective between inner and outer worlds is also reminiscent of Novalis, who seeks to establish such a union:

Wir müssen suchen eine innere Welt zu schaffen, die eigentlicher Pendant der äussren Welt ist, die, in dem sie ihr auf allen Punkten bestimmt entgegengesetzt wird, unsere Freiheit immer mehr erweitert.[25]

Rilke, living a century after Novalis, is a neoromantic: "Rilke ist nach seinem Allerlebnis, auch seiner Erfahrung überräumlicher und überzeitlicher Verbindungen *ein Romantiker,* ein Fortsetzer der deutschen Innerlichkeit . . . er ist es auch mit seiner Sehnsucht nach Transzendenz. . . ."[26]

Finally the bridge is a symbol for Rilke's poetic mind establishing an artistic harmony over external chaos—over the "wirre Wege" and that which travels in endless circles. The bridge becomes a passage to the realm of art, which is permanent ("das immer gleiche"), unerringly valid ("der unbewegliche Gerechte"), and which provides identity ("Markstein") and access to the essence of all things ("der dunkle Eingang . . ."). The blind man, himself a member of the physical world, is unable to see that which "irrt und rinnt und prunkt," and thus turns his view inward to the ordered realm of art where he can attain a final composure and serenity.

9

Ernst Stadler: Fahrt über die Kölner Rheinbrücke bei Nacht"

Fahrt über die Kölner Rheinbrücke bei Nacht

Der Schnellzug tastet sich und stösst die Dunkelheit entlang.
Kein Stern will vor. Die ganze Welt ist nur ein enger, nachtum-
    schienter Minengang,
Darein zuweilen Förderstellen blauen Lichtes jähe Horizonte
    reissen: Feuerkreis
Von Kugellampen, Dächern, Schloten, dampfend, strömend . . .
    nur sekundenweis . . .
Und wieder alles schwarz. Als führen wir ins Eingeweid der
    Nacht zur Schicht.
Nun taumeln Lichter her . . . verirrt, trostlos vereinsamt . . .
    mehr . . . und sammeln sich . . . und werden dicht.
Gerippe grauer Häuserfronten liegen bloss, im Zwielicht blei-
    chend, tot—etwas muss kommen . . . o, ich fühl es schwer
Im Hirn. Eine Beklemmung singt im Blut. Dann dröhnt der
    Boden plötzlich wie ein Meer:

Wir fliegen, aufgehoben, königlich durch nachtentrissne Luft,
hoch übern Strom. O Biegung der Millionen Lichter, stumme
Wacht,
Vor deren blitzender Parade schwer die Wasser abwärts rollen.
Endloses Spalier, zum Gruss gestellt bei Nacht!
Wie Fackeln stürmend! Freudiges! Salut von Schiffen über
blauer See! Bestirntes Fest!
Wimmelnd, mit hellen Augen hingedrängt! Bis wo die Stadt mit
letzten Häusern ihren Gast entlässt.
Und dann die langen Einsamkeiten. Nackte Ufer. Stille. Nacht.
Besinnung. Einkehr. Kommunion. Und Glut und Drang
Zum Letzten, Segnenden. Zum Zeugungsfest. Zur Wollust. Zum
Gebet. Zum Meer. Zum Untergang.

"Fahrt über die Kölner Rheinbrücke bei Nacht," written
by Ernst Stadler in 1913, uses the passage of an express
train across a bridge to convey the poet's inner condition.
The objectivity of the title is in contrast to the highly lyrical
content and remains the only factual statement of the poem.
Stadler combines dithyrambic lines with short verse fragments to form an affirmation of life and death in face of
a pessimistic world.

The very opening line demonstrates a divergence from
the objectivity of the title. It offers imagery rather than
description: "Der Schnellzug tastet sich und stösst die
Dunkelheit entlang." The train becomes an animate being
groping and searching in the night. The alliterative s sound
emphasizes the steady, relentless thrust of the train against
the darkness: "Der Schellzug tastet sich and stösst die Dunkelheit entlang." Stadler's use of the train as a metaphor for
his own condition becomes evident as the poem progresses.

The second line expands the setting from the train to
the sky above: "Kein Stern will vor." The stars do not
penetrate the darkness; the world is devoid of the light
provided by nature. The verse emphasizes the blackness in
which the train is groping and introduces the negative
element that dominates the first part of the poem. The

absence of the stars suggests the absence of any transcending values to oppose the gloominess of the scene.

In the second line the poet expands his view to form an image of the entire world: "Die ganze Welt ist nur ein enger, nachtumschienter Minengang. . . ." "Eng" defines the world narrowed by the absence of the stars, and "nur" further limits these boundaries. "Nachtumschienter" reiterates the pervasive darkness of the realm in which the train moves. The second part of the word ("nacht*umschienter*") —literally "railed around"—indicates the confined condition of the world yet felicitously remains within the context of the initial image, the train. "Minengang," a tunnel in which explosives are stored, again implies the narrowness and limitation of the world and indicates the potential danger to those within its confines.

The following two lines continue to expand Stadler's view of the world:

Darein zuweilen Förderstellen blauen Lichtes jähe Horizonte
   reissen: Feuerkreis
Von Kugellampen, Dächern, Schloten, dampfend, strömend . . .
   nur sekundenweis. . . .

Although the natural light of the stars is absent from the world, artificial light ("Förderstellen blauen Lichtes") flashes intermittently in the darkness. "Förderstellen" and "Schnellzug" indicate a mechanized world of technology. These flashes form "sudden horizons," an ironic image since the horizon should derive its light from the sun and not from technology. The rapid sequence of objects ("Kugellampen . . . Dächern . . . Schloten . . .") and "strömend" evoke the speed of the train. The convulsive nature of the technological world is indicated with "reissen." Industrial factories are suggested in the smoke issuing from chimneys: "Dächern, Schloten, dampfend. . . ." The random mixture of nouns and participles implies an aimless, disjointed world. In contrast to the continuous glow of stars, the artificial lights appear "zuweilen" and "nur sekundenweis" in the darkness: the technological realm is characterized by evanescence rather than permanence. The momentary flashes of light are reproduced syntactically with the fragmentary ". . . nur sekundenweis. . . ." Finally there is a regression to the blackness of night indicated at the beginning of the poem: "und wieder alles schwarz." The finality of "und wieder alles schwarz" emphasizes the inescapable dreariness of the technology enclosing man.

In the following line Stadler alludes to the men within this technological world: "Als führen wir ins Eingeweid der Nacht zur Schicht." The poet now imposes himself on the outer world with his use of *wir*. "Eingeweid der Nacht" is a restatement of "nachtumschienter Minengang." The night remains all-pervasive. Yet "Eingeweid der Nacht" is a more unpleasant image than "nachtumschienter Minengang." It also implies a limited world confining man, yet one containing inert, visceral matter. "Zur Schicht," in context with the "Minengang" of the second line as well as "Eingeweid der Nacht," projects a negative image of miners on the way to their shift.

The darkness is again interrupted by light as the train continues its journey. Once more there is not the serene, natural light of the stars, but a chaotic medley of artificial lights:

Nun *taumeln* Lichter her . . . *verirrt,* trostlos vereinsamt . . . mehr . . . und sammeln sich . . . und werden dicht. (italics added)

The lights do not provide aid or guidance in the darkness, but are themselves lost and isolated, much like the groping train. There is dramatic intensification as the lights multiply and grow dense, indicating the progress of the train as it emerges from the tunnel and continues toward the bridge. The juxtaposition of fragments indicates the ever-greater number of lights yet also accentuates the greater despair and loneliness that result:

> trostlos vereinsamt . . .
> mehr . . . und sammeln sich . . . und werden dicht.

This intensified anxiety hardly reaches a climax. The light that is produced only helps to underscore the pervading desolation and hopelessness. Verbs of motion ("taumeln, sammeln sich") are replaced by the stagnant *"liegen* bloss." That which has been shrouded in darkness appears lifeless:

> Gerippe grauer Häuserfronten liegen bloss, im
> Zwielicht bleichend, tot—. . . .

The light of this line ("Zwielicht") is the light within the houses of the city. The illuminated windows make the houses appear as skeletons, as pale ("bleichend"), naked façades ("liegen bloss, Häuser*fronten*"). These drab skeletons manifest the lifelessness of the city (". . . im Zwielicht bleichend, *tot*—. . ."). "Gerippe" carries an equally negative anatomical connotation as the workers go into the entrails ("Eingeweid") of night to work their shifts. A bleak picture is painted of man and the city in which he lives.

"Tot" concludes the first part of the poem and characterizes the view of the world presented. The express train has passed from darkness through light and back into darkness. The final tumult of lights only helps to reveal the nakedness and futility within the city. Into this pessimistic view Stadler's poetic *ich* intervenes. It breaks through the chaos and anticipates a new order: "—etwas muss kommen . . . o, ich fühl es schwer / Im Hirn." It now becomes evident that the searching and anticipation of the train in the first verse ("Der Schnellzug tastet sich und stösst die Dunkelheit entlang.") reflect the search of the poetic *ich,* which until now has confronted only oppression and desolation. The accumulation of lights and appearance of the naked house fronts described the poet's anxiety and consequent depression. The "etwas" that the poet anticipates promises a new optimism, as indicated in the verb: "Eine Beklemmung *singt* im Blut." No longer do discordant verbs such as "reissen," "taumeln," or "verirren" appear. "Singt" indicates an element of harmony in the confusion and hopelessness. Anatomical imagery no longer evokes oppression ("Eingeweid") and death ("Gerippe"). "Hirn" and "Blut" imply life of the poet's mind and body and his potential to surmount the chaos he glimpses.

As the train leaves the edge of the city and enters the bridge, there is a sudden roar, signifying Stadler's emancipation from all confining limitations: "Dann dröhnt der Boden plötzlich wie ein Meer." The sea suggests an open expanse of space, which is in contrast to the "enger, nachtumschienter Minengang" of the world in the first part of the poem. The sea is also a manifestation of nature, which was absent from the technological realm ("Kein Stern will vor.") "Wie ein Meer" indicates the poet's capability of forming similes now with nature rather than with the oppressive industrial realm ("Als führen wir ins Eingeweid der Nacht zur Schicht.") The bridge passes over the river, which symbolizes the natural flow of life. The train becomes figuratively and literally a vehicle to bring the poet into contact with life.[1]

In the following verse the collective *wir* reappears. Again Stadler embosses his lyrical *ich* on the outer world, but no longer does the former oppression appear ("Als führen *wir* ins Eingeweid der Nacht zur Schicht"). The verse rather suggests joy and transport:

> Wir fliegen, anfgehoben, königlich durch nachtentrissne
> Luft, hoch übern Strom.

"Fliegen" and "aufgehoben" suggest a transcendence of the chaotic world depicted in the first part of the poem. The bridge symbolizes passage from disorder to the harmony as anticipated in "singt." No longer is the poet confined within the darkness. His spirit is freed from the oppressive "Eingeweid der Nacht." "Nacht*umschienter*" is now replaced by "nacht*entrissne*," indicating the poet's emancipation from the night. "Wir" no longer represents the worker, but the emancipated spirit. "Hoch übern Strom" emphasizes the poet's transcendence of his previous environment, described as "dampfend, *strömend*." "Königlich" indicates man's new status; he is no longer oppressed but, in his newly attained freedom, is under his own sovereignty.

The tone of the poem now becomes hymnic as the poet rejoices in the flood of lights emanating from the bridge:

O Biegung der Millionen Lichter,
Stumme Wacht,

Vor deren blitzender Parade schwer die Wasser abwärts rollen.
Endloses Spalier, zum Gruss gestellt bei Nacht!

The lights of the bridge stand out to beckon and greet man in the darkness. Unlike the lights in the first part of the poem, they are not scattered and isolated but appear harmoniously in an arc ("Biegung") that outlines the bridge's superstructure. They do not serve to confuse an already chaotic world but function as a sentinel to provide guidance and assistance to those in the darkness. Although it too is a product of man's technology, the bridge symbolizes a redeeming rather than a destructive aspect of the modern world. The poem itself is like a bridge, which Stadler constructs to show his sovereignty over chaos and hopelessness. The bridge serves as a symbol to ennoble man rather than disgrace him (e.g., "Als führen wir ins Eingeweid der Nacht"). It becomes a technological savior of man that rejoins him with nature.

"Blitzender Parade" indicates the festive atmosphere created by the glittering lights that replace the "jähe Horizonte" earlier in the poem. In contrast to the pessimism of the workers passing through the entrails of night, optimism now prevails in a joyful parade of celebration. The transcending height of this festival is emphasized as the waters appear to roll downward from the high vantage point of the bridge (". . . schwer die Wasser abwärts rollen"). The regularity suggested in "rollen" forms a contrast to the convulsive "reissen" and unsteady "taumeln" earlier in the poem. "Rollen" also characterizes the verse cadence of the second part; no longer are there interruptions (e.g., ". . . nur sekundenweis . . .") or discordant mixtures of parts of speech (e.g., "Dächern, Schloten, dampfend, strömend . . ."). This new world is without bounds, as suggested in "wie ein Meer" and now again with "*Endloses* Spalier." Its infinite reaches contrast with "*enger* nachtumschienter Minengang" as well as with the transience of "zuweilen" and "nur sekundenweis." "Spalier," a squad of guards forming a lane with crossed swords overhead, is suggested by the steelwork of the bridge. Like "stumme Wacht," this squad protects those who enter the bridge from the darkness. The bridge is a greeting to those coming upon it in the chaos of existence: "Zum Gruss gestellt bei Nacht!"

The excitement and jubilation of the poet's soul here become evident with a series of exclamation points:

> Endloses Spalier, zum Gruss gestellt bei Nacht!
> Wie Fackeln stürmend! Freudiges! Salut von Schiffen über
>   blauer See! Bestirntes Fest!
> Wimmelnd, mit hellen Augen hingedrängt!

The death of the first part of the poem now becomes a festival of life, as symbolized by the river passing under the bridge. The poet's joy comes to a climax as he is transported beyond all limits in revelry. A spiritual rapture is achieved, the one- and two-word exclamations suggesting the intensity of his joy. Lights now overwhelm the poet as he is enkindled with joy and new life: "Wie Fackeln stürmend." No longer do chaotic bursts of light tumble forward to reveal death and hopelessness; the despair of "trostlos vereinsamt" now becomes the rapture of "Freudiges!" The greeting accorded by the bridge ("Zum Gruss gestellt bei Nacht") is reciprocated by the ships at sea. Loneliness and isolation are replaced by communion and salutation: "Salut von Schiffen über blauer See!" "Über blauer See" emphasizes the pervasiveness of the bridge's influence as a guiding beacon. The poet here uses symbols of life and nature to reflect the new life of his artistic inspiration. "Blauer See" associates the color blue with nature rather than artificiality ("Förderstellen *blauen* Lichtes"). In contrast to the initial scene of darkness where no star appears ("Kein *Stern* will vor"), the lights of the bridge are seen as a starred festival ("Be*stirntes* Fest!"). Point for point, Stadler's previous pessimism turns to optimism as his spirit is regenerated. Teeming lights replace the darkness: "Wimmelnd, mit hellen Augen hingedrängt!" "Helle Augen" oppose the darkness of "nachtumschienter Minengang" and the gloominess of "*grauer* Häuserfronten . . .in *Zwielicht* bleichend" and present another positive element in Stadler's repertoire of anatomical imagery. "Helle Augen" restate the function of the bridge as a "stumme Wacht" to watch all who enter and protect them from the darkness. "Hingedrängt" refers to the poet, who continues to be transported into the spiritual realm by the brightness of the bridge. No longer must he actively push the darkness along ("stösst die Dunkelheit entlang") but is passively borne by the ecstasy reflected in the bright lights.

"Hingedrängt" concludes the second part of the poem and stands in contrast to "tot," which ends the first part. Stadler has found the impetus and inspiration to seek further. No longer is he searching confusedly in the darkness, feeling his way ("tastet sich") with each step, since he is on the path toward finding his goal, the "etwas" that is described in the conclusion of the poem:

> . . . Bis wo die Stadt mit
> letzten Häusern ihren Gast entlässt.
> Und dann die langen Einsamkeiten. Nackte Ufer. Stille. Nacht.
> Besinnung. Einkehr. Kommunion. Und Glut und Drang
> Zum Letzten, Segnenden. Zum Zeugungsfest. Zur Wollust.
> Zum Gebet. Zum Meer. Zum Untergang.

The excited tempo of the second part now subsides as the express passes over the bridge and out into the lonely stretches of the countryside. Stadler now reflects on the insights he has gained. The city and its skeletal façades are left behind: ". . . Bis wo die Stadt mit letzten Häusern ihren Gast entlässt." Once again the scenery reflects the state of the poet's mind—a figurative bridge has been established between inner and outer realms. Just as the flashing blue lights and the dead house fronts represented chaos and desolation and as the bridge and river offered transport and regeneration, so the long, lonely stretches ("die langen Einsamkeiten") and the bare banks ("Nackte Ufer") now represent reflection, meditation, and stillness ("Stille . . . Besinnung. Einkehr.") The darkness of night returns ("Nacht"), but it is not a darkness interrupted by intermittent flashes of light, but a darkness of introspection and meditation. The poet's language here suggests religious sanctity. "Kommunion" indicates the spiritual fulfillment that Stadler has attained and is in direct contrast to "trostlos vereinsamt" in the first part of the poem. The poet has now achieved an inner calm ("Stille") as well as a sense of purpose and conviction ("Drang") in life. Passage over the bridge has given him spiritual guidance and direction, "Zum Letzten, Segnenden." He has been liberated from the fetters of the limited technological world, which served only to confuse and obfuscate the "etwas" that he had been seeking in the darkness. The intoxication of the long dithyrambic verses now becomes release and satiation through single words, as the poet anticipates blissful dissolution in the river of life.

Stadler's fulfillment is described in sensual and erotic as well as spiritual terms: "Zum Zeugungsfest. Zur Wollust." Total consummation of life as well as death includes physical satisfaction and fulfillment. "Zeugungsfest" recalls the celebration of "Bestirntes Fest." "Zum Gebet" recalls "Kommunion" and "Segnenden" and again emphasizes the religious aspect of Stadler's experience. With "Zum Meer. Zum Untergang" this experience becomes complete as the poet lets the universe embrace his spirit. The sea, referred to twice before ("Dann dröhnt der Boden plötzlich wie ein Meer . . . ;" "Salut von Schiffen über blauer See!"), signified expansion, which opposed the confinement of *enger, nacht-umschienter* Minengang. . . ." The sea also is the body of water receiving the Rhine river. Just as the Rhine terminates its existence by flowing into the sea, so the poet's life proceeds toward extinction in the figurative sea of the universe ("Zum Meer. Zum Untergang"). Stadler no longer views death negatively, as in the first part of the poem. "Zum Meer. Zum Untergang." emphasizes death as a natural process and a final release from the restrictions of the world. The "Kölner Rheinbrücke," in the final analysis, is the bridge from the outer world to the inner self, from confusion and futility to harmony and purpose, and from life to death.

The bridge holds significance for Stadler, because it provides him with an optimistic rather than pessimistic view of death. It spans the river, which offers the inspiration of nature rather than the oppression of the city. And finally, the symbol of the bridge represents the poet's ability to attain an artistic sovereignty ("aufgehoben . . . königlich") over a chaotic world.

10

Gottfried Benn:
"Am Brückenwehr"

Am Brückenwehr

I.

"Ich habe weit gedacht.
nun lasse ich die Dinge
und löse ihre Ringe
der neuen Macht.

Gelehnt am Brückenwehr
die hellen Wasser rauschen
die Elemente tauschen
sich hin und her.

Der Lauf ist schiefergrau,
der Ton der Urgesteine,
als noch das Land alleine
im Schichtenbau.

Des Sommers Agonie
gibt auch ein Rebgehänge,
Kelter- und Weingesänge
durchstreifen sie.

Wessen ist das und wer?
Dessen, der alles machte,
dessen, der es dann dachte
vom Ende her?

Ich habe weit gedacht,
ich lebte in Gedanken,
bis ihre Häupter sanken
vor welcher Macht?"

II.

"Vor keiner Macht zu sinken,
vor keinem Rausch zur Ruh,
du selbst bist Trank und Trinken,
der Denker, du.

Du bist ja nicht der Hirte
und ziehst nicht mit Schalmein,
wenn der, wie du, sich irrte,
ist nie Verzeihn.

Du bist ja nicht der Jäger
aus Megalith und Ur,
du bist der Formenpräger
der weissen Spur.

So viele sind vergangen
im Bach—und Brückenschein,
wer kennt nicht das Verlangen
zum Urgestein—:

Doch dir bestimmt: kein Werden,
du bleibst gebannt und bist
der Himmel und der Erden
Formalist.

Du kannst es keinem zeigen
und keinem du entfliehn,
du trägst durch Nacht und Schweigen
den Denker—ihn."

III.

"Doch wenn dann Stunden sind,
wo ohne Rang und Reue
das Alte und das Neue
zusammenrinnt,

wo ohne Unterschied
das Wasser und die Welle,
das Dunkle und das Helle
das eine Lied,

ein Lied, des Stimme rief
gegen Geschichtsgewalten
das in sich selbst Gestalten
asiatisch tief—

ach, wenn die Stunden dann kommen
und dichter werden und mehr
Sommer und Jahre verglommen,
singt man am Brückenwehr:

lass mich noch einmal reich sein,
wie es die Jugend gedacht,
lass mich noch einmal weich sein
im Blumengeruch der Nacht,

nimm mir die Hölle, die Hülle,
die Form, den Formungstrieb,
gib mir die Tiefe, die Fülle,
die Schöpfung—gib!"

IV.

"Bist du auf Grate gestiegen
sahst du die Gipfel klar:
Adler, die wirklichen, fliegen
schweigend und unfruchtbar.

Kürzer steht es in Früchten,
früher, dass es verblich,
nahe am Schöpfer züchten
wenige Arten sich.

Ewig schweigend das Blaue,
wer noch an Stimmen denkt,
hat schon den Blick, die Braue
wieder in Sehnsucht gesenkt.

Du aber dienst Gestalten
über dem Brückenwehr,
über den stumpfen Gewalten
Völker und Schnee und Meer:

formen, das ist deine Fülle,
der Rasse auferlegt,
formen, bis die Hülle
die ganze Tiefe trägt,

die Hülle wird dann zeigen,
und keiner kann entfliehn,
dass Form und Tiefe Reigen,
durch den die Adler ziehn."

Gottfried Benn's "Am Brückenwehr," written in 1934, one year after Hitler came to power, represents a self-dialogue that scrutinizes the poet's thinking and function as an artist. By this time Benn had rejected all affiliation with the Third Reich and had recognized that his former dreams of uniting intellect and politics could not be realized: "Es sind zwei Reiche," he wrote in a letter to Ina Seidel in

September of 1934. "Am Brückenwehr" marks Benn's turn
from politics to art and looks forward to his future course as
a writer.[1] Benn realized that only in the realm of art could
the synthesis of opposites, which had failed in political life,
be achieved.

Benn begins his poem in a contemplative pose. The poet
stands at the parapet of a bridge and observes the flowing
waters below him. The first stanza introduces the poet's
resolution to turn away from all restraints limiting his
existence:

> "Ich habe weit gedacht,
> nun lasse ich die Dinge
> und löse ihre Ringe
> der neuen Macht."

Benn renounces "die Dinge," all ontological phenomena. He
releases "ihre Ringe," the rational connections that lead in
endless circles, and finally leaves them in favor of an intangible "neue Macht," the true nature of which is not revealed
until later in the poem.

The second stanza symbolizes Benn's passage from the
"Dinge" to "der neuen Macht" with the image of the bridge:

> "Gelehnt am Brückenwehr
> die hellen Wasser rauschen
> die Elemente tauschen
> sich hin und her."

The brightness ("hellen") of the rushing water attracts the
poet's eye. It draws his attention to the activity below,
thereby diverting him from the "Ringe" of reality. "Hell"
also suggests the lucid, creative state of the poet's mind,
which has escaped the stagnation inherent in "ich habe weit
gedacht." Whereas the "Denken" of his former existence
remained unproductive and confined to "Ringen," "rauschen" and "tauschen" imply activity, flux, and even
Dionysian intoxication. It is in this activity experienced in
nature that Benn discovers a recourse from the problems

confronting him. "Elemente," the simplest forms constituting nature, imply the breakdown ("lösen") of all that which had formerly been unresolvable "Dinge." The liquid sounds of "lasse," "löse," "gelehnt," "hellen," and "Elemente" emphasize the poet's fascination with the water and its power to dissolve all bonds. "Rauschen" and "hin und her" imply a lack of order in contrast to the symmetry implied in "Ringe"—Benn now allows his senses to rule him rather than the logicality of his thought processes ("weit gedacht"). "Hin und her" also suggests the potential of the river to carry the poet back and forth in the flow of time, a thought that occupies the two following stanzas.

The simplicity that Benn experiences in the elements appears in the primeval description of the third stanza. The "schiefergrau" water of the river transports the poet back in time ("hin") to a primitive landscape barren of organic life:

> "Der Lauf ist schiefergrau
> der Ton der Urgesteine,
> als noch das Land alleine
> im Schichtenbau."

"Urgesteine" indicates the poet's regression to a primordial world of nature. "Schichtenbau" (stratification) is reminiscent of "Elemente" in its reduction of nature to its composite structure. "Allein" underscores this rudimentary condition, and simultaneously reflects the newly found seclusion of the poet from the "Dinge" of reality.

This primitive world is contrasted with the joy and celebration of life in the fourth stanza. The poet is carried forward in time ("her") to an autumnal view of life:

> "Des Sommers Agonie
> gibt auch ein Rebgehänge,
> Kelter—und Weingesänge
> durchstreifen sie."

Nature here again provides the poet with a visionary release from the strictures of reality. The "schiefergrau" rock strata

are replaced by colorful images of Bacchic pleasure: "Rebgehänge, Kelter- und Weingesänge." Benn now envisions the
emotional aspect of life ("rauschen"), which offers emancipation from all factors limiting his existence.

Yet the vision that the poet sees reflected in the "hin
und her" of the river fails to explain the true nature of
"der neuen Macht." Although Benn has abandoned all
"Dinge" and is led to an intimation of the mysterious new
power, his dual experience of nature (primeval and modern)
precipitates a series of questions regarding the creator of
these things. Thus the poet must figuratively remain poised
on the bridge, contemplating and seeking solutions regarding
the existence of man and God:

> "Wessen ist das und wer?
> Dessen, der alles machte,
> dessen, der es dann dachte
> vom Ende her?"

The two questions ask whether the world belongs to God
("Dessen, der alles machte") or to man ("dessen, der es dann
dachte / vom Ende her?"), who as a late appearance on
earth can only cognitively comprehend its essence. "Wessen
ist das und wer?" recalls the poet's quandary of the first
stanza ("Ich habe weit gedacht, nun lasse ich die Dinge")
and leads him back into the realm of thought. "Wessen ist
das . . . ," however, now questions the origin of "der neuen
Macht," which remains elusively hidden in the exchange
of elements.

The final stanza underscores the seriousness of Benn's
dilemma. No solution is proffered and his thoughts remain
powerless:

> "Ich habe weit gedacht,
> ich lebte in Gedanken,
> bis ihre Häupter sanken
> vor welcher Macht?"

Benn's attempt to release himself from the rings of reality
has only succeeded in a momentary vision. "Ich habe weit
gedacht" repeats the first line of the poem to indicate the
circular path ("Ring") leading the poet back to the beginning
of his quandary. "Ich lebte in Gedanken" is essentially a
restatement of "Ich habe weit gedacht," but provides added
emphasis to Benn's predicament. The poet is unable to
utilize his thought processes ("weit gedacht . . . Gedanken"),
either to answer the questions of the fifth stanza or to
discover the true nature of the "neuen Macht." Such inca-
pability forces the figurative heads of Benn's thoughts
("Gedanken . . . ihre Häupter") to bow themselves in
bewilderment before the undiscovered power. The first
quartet must end in perplexity with an unresolved question
("vor welcher Macht?"). The poet is thwarted and admits
his mental impotence. Yet his open question reveals a
continued desire to discover and understand the mysterious
power confronting him.

This mood of discouragement is reversed in the second
part of the poem with a self-injunction severely critical of
resignation. This critical objectivity is attained with a *du*
address rather than the lyrical *ich*. The use of "sinken"
establishes a continuity between quartets while simultaneously contrasting the attitudes of the two speakers: the
ich of the poet is disconsolate, yet the *du* remains firm:

> ". . . bis ihre Häupter *sanken*
> vor keinem Rausch zur Ruh,
>
> "Vor keiner Macht zu *sinken*,
> vor keinem Rausch zur Ruh,
> du selbst bist Trank und Trinken
> der Denker, du."

Benn castigates himself for subjugating the powers of his
mind to those of the "neuen Macht." The stanza represents
an assertion of the ego: "vor keiner Macht zu sinken. . . ."
It must not let itself be overcome by the creative "Rausch"

("vor keinem Rausch zur Ruh . . .") as before in part I ("die hellen Wasser rauschen") and linger complacently in such a mood ("Ruh"), but be ever conscious that in its state of solitude it must depend entirely on itself. In this way "Trank und Trinken" becomes an image for circular, self-nourishing self-consciousness, for the *du* constitutes the process of imbibing ("Trinken") that which the poet himself is ("Trank"). Again the key words of the stanza are alliterated to provide added emphasis: "*R*ausch zur *R*uh . . . *T*rank und *T*rinken. . . ." The alliterated *d* of "*d*er *D*enker, *du*" is reminiscent of "*d*essen, *d*er es *d*ann *d*achte vom Ende her" (I, 5); in both verses the subject is the thinker, yet now he is viewed as self-reliant rather than helpless.

In the second and third stanzas Benn continues to emphasize his role as thinker. He contrasts himself, a modern man, to the shepherd and hunter of a more primitive civilization:

> "Du bist ja nicht der Hirte
> und ziehst nicht mit Schalmein,
> wenn der, wie du, sich irrte,
> ist nie Verzeihn.
>
> Du bist ja nicht der Jäger
> aus Megalith und Ur,
> du bist der Formenpräger
> der weissen Spur."

"Schalmein," like "Weingesänge," uses a musical image to convey the emotional and idyllic aspect of life opposing the reality of "Dinge" and the logic of "Ringe." Yet this idyllic, pastoral image of the shepherd is not left unqualified. He too, like Benn, is never destined to find forgiveness:

> ". . . wenn der, wie du, sich irrte
> ist nie Verzeihn."

The present tense apodosis ("ist nie Verzeihn") to a past condition ("sich irrte") suggests universality and timeless meaning, and therefore the unforgiven "Hirte" as Christ. Thus Benn once more, as with his vision in the first part of the poem, undermines his idyll by submitting it to the scrutiny of the critical mind.

The hunter in the following stanza provides a parallel image to the shepherd. Similar verse structure emphasizes this parallel:

> "Du bist ja nicht der Hirte . . .
> Du bist ja nicht der Jäger. . . .

Yet in this stanza the poet draws a contrast rather than a comparison with his subject. These verses reflect Benn's political rather than his moral self. He perceives himself as separate from the hunter and the ancient peoples (e.g., in the ancient Sumerian city of Ur) who erected huge prehistoric monuments of stone ("Megalith"). As such, he holds himself aloof from Hitler's genealogical obsession with the ancient heritage of the German peoples, and also rejects his own "Aryan" ancestry, which he had proved earlier in 1934.[2] Now he is convinced that it is the artist's primary task to be a "Formenpräger," a view of art that the Nazi regime consistently opposed. "Weisse Spur," the Caucasian race, refers to Benn's identification with modern Western civilization in general and not Germany in particular. The white race is no longer close to nature as were the primitive peoples, but is identified by Benn with cultivated and formalistic art. As Benn states in his essay "Pallas" (1943): "Der weisse letzte [Mensch] ist nicht mehr Natur. . . . Sein Ziel, mag sein nur sein Übergang, jedenfalls sein existentieller Auftrag lautet nicht mehr natürliche Natur, sondern bearbeitete Natur, gedankliche Natur, stilisierte Natur—Kunst" (929).

The fourth stanza marks again a change of moods and once again acknowledges desire to return to a primitive culture, except that now the desire appears universal rather than individual. The poet has succeeded in objectifying his position of the first quartet:

> "So viele sind vergangen
> im Bach- und Brückenschein,
> wer kennt nicht das Verlangen
> zum Urgestein—:"

Once more the images of the bridge and river appear. "Bach-schein" is a repetition of "die *hellen* Wasser" in the first part of the poem. The river becomes now a symbol of evanescent life, which flows toward the sea of the absolute (this sea appears in the "Meer" of part IV, 4), and the bridge reflects the transition from life to death as well as from present to past ("wer kennt nicht das Verlangen zum Urgestein?").

The hyphen at the end of the fourth stanza signifies a sudden interruption of the poet's reverie. In the fifth stanza Benn goes on to reject the "Verlangen nach Urgestein" as a seductive vision of primordial unity that diverts him from his commitment to formalistic art:

> "Doch dir bestimmt: kein Werden,
> du bleibst gebannt und bist
> der Himmel und der Erden
> Formalist."

The poet denies himself organic participation ("kein Werden") in the development of mankind from the ancient peoples forward. Such participation would be a mistake. He must segregate himself from all that is transitory to become a universal representative of not only the earth, but also heaven ("Himmel und Erden"). He sees himself as bound ("gebannt" is reminiscent of "Ringen") to his task as an artist, as a "Formalist." "Formalist" comprises an entire verse to provide emphasis and finality, as well as to underscore the aloofness of the poet.

The last verses of the stanza restate and reaffirm the poet's self-determination of the first stanza. He must remain alone in his quest for artistic sovereignty ("Du kannst es keinem zeigen"), but on the other hand he is not free of human responsibilities and frailties ("keinem du entfliehen"). Nevertheless, he will remain resolute in his aspiration to become poet and thinker even though his creative endeavor must exist in a rarefied atmosphere. "Nacht und Schweigen" appear as opposites to the metaphors of life ("die hellen Wasser," "Bach- und Brückenschein," "Weingesänge," "Schalmein"), and emphasize again Benn's turn away from political and historical events. In the final verse the poet objectifies the intellect within himself to emphasize the cool aloofness of the "Formalist": "der Denker, *du*" becomes "du trägst . . . den Denker—*ihn.*"

But the third part of the poem represents yet another renewal of Benn's desire for metaphysical dissolution of all boundaries that he still perceives to confine him. "Doch" introduces the quartet and signifies the contrast to be drawn with the formalistic commitment in part II:

> "Doch wenn dann Stunden sind,
> wo ohne Rang und Reue
> das Alte und das Neue
> zusammenrinnt. . . ."

The renewed quotation marks and the absence of *du* indicate a situation parallel to the first part of the poem. Benn now again contemplates the periods of emotional intoxication, when all antitheses are integrated. He then considers himself free from the strictures of position and order ("Rang" is reminiscent of "Ring") as well as the remorse and repentance that hold man in abeyance ("ohne Reue" is a contrast to "keinem du entfliehen"). The primitive and the modern ("Das Alte und das Neue") combine to form a continuity. "Zusammenrinnt" is itself composed of two words that "run together" to form a new meaning. The bridge, still the place of the poet's meditation, is recalled in all of these images to indicate synthesis and unity.

The second stanza continues the combination of opposites by using images that the poet glimpses from the bridge:

> ". . . wo ohne Unterschied
> das Wasser und die Welle,

> das Dunkle und das Helle
> das eine Lied. . . ."

The "Wasser," a substance, is amorphous and no different
from the "Welle" that suggests form and surface. This synthesis is strengthened by the alliterative *d* and *w* ("*d*as
*W*asser und *d*ie Welle.") The "Dunkle" characterizing the
world of "der Denker" ("*Nacht* und Schweigen") is combined with "das Helle," which characterizes the world of
nature and the spirit ("die *hellen* Wasser rauschen"). Each
opposite is reconciled as a component of an overall harmony—"das eine Lied." "Lied" recalls the musical images of
"Weingesänge" and "Schalmein," both attributes of the
primitive past.

The third stanza elaborates on this "Lied":

> ". . . ein Lied, des Stimme rief
> gegen Geschichtsgewalten
> das in sich selbst Gestalten
> asiatisch tief—"

The voice of the song does not evoke historical events, which
are temporal or diachronic in nature, but rather brings forth
figures that are connected with the Oriental philosophy of
timelessness ("asiatisch tief"). Benn states in "Zur Problematik des Dichterischen" (1930) that the poet is one who is
dissolved in the shadow of antiquity, where "das Ich ist
dunkler, als das Jahrhundert dachte" (642). Such hours
evoke different images from those created by the formalist.
They bring forth forms ("in sich selbst Gestalten") that
appear mythical and dreamlike and are connected with
man's collective unconscious. As Benn further remarks in
"Problematik," "Von weither liegt in ihm ein Traum, ein
Tier, von weither ist er mit Mysterien beladen, von jenen
frühen Völkern her, die noch die Urzeit, den Ursprung in
sich trugen, mit ihrem uns so völlig fremden Weltgefühl . . ."
(643). After transcending the confines of body and consciousness, the poet acquires the depth reflected in "asiatisch tief."
Again Benn states, "Der Körper ist der letzte Zwang und die

Tiefe der Notwendigkeit, er trägt die Ahnung, er träumt den Traum" (643).

With this mood, which evokes depth rather than form, a new and less energetic verse structure is introduced as dactyls take the place of the shorter iambic verses:

"ach, wenn die Stunden dann kommen
und dichter werden und mehr
Sommer und Jahre verglommen,
singt man am Brückenwehr: . . ."

"Ach" expresses the emotion that seizes the poet and separates him from his task as formalist. "Wenn dann Stunden kommen" reiterates the first verse of the quartet to introduce a new flow of sentiment. "Und dichter werden" indicates the accelerated passage of time after all boundaries are suspended and implies emergence of the "Dichter," the poet. "Und mehr Sommer und Jahre verglommen," like a former verse ("ein Lied, des Stimme rief gegen Geschichtsgewalten"), emphasizes the disappearance of all temporal limitations.

The poet glimpses a harmony enabling him to "sing" his "Lied." "Singt" refers not only to "Lied" but also to the previous musical images suggestive of emotion ("Weingesänge"; "Schalmein"). Once more the image of the bridge is used ("singt man am Brückenwehr") to connect figuratively the realm of "Form" with the realm of "Tiefe," for which the poet now longs:

". . . lass mich noch einmal reich sein.
wie es die Jugend gedacht,
lass mich noch einmal weich sein
im Blumengeruch der Nacht,

nimm mir die Hölle, die Hülle,
die Form, den Formungstrieb,
gib mir die Tiefe, die Fülle,
die Schöpfung—gib!"

The urgency of the poet's desire for depth and a fuller enrichment of life is revealed in the five-fold use of the imperative. He asks for a regression into childhood, an escape from the present to the simple existence; as Harald Steinhagen comments: "Sehnsucht nach Kindheit, in dem Ich und Welt noch nicht einander entfremdet waren."[3] "Weich" opposes the rigid qualities of the "Formalist," who remains "bestimmt" and "gebannt." "Blumengeruch" emphasizes the use of the senses rather than the intellect. The "Hülle," the prior formalistic devotion of the poet, now reveals itself as a "Hölle" from which Benn longs for emancipation. The assonance and alliteration of "Hölle/Hülle" and "Form/Formungstrieb" impart a musical quality to the stanza that opposes the rigidity of the "Formalist." "Nimm mir . . . ," comprising the first two verses, is balanced by "gib mir," comprising the final two. "Fülle" and "Hülle" oppose one another as do "Wasser" and "Welle" in the first stanza. Benn appeals for "Tiefe" (seen before in the third stanza as "asiatisch tief—") to counteract the shallowness of form. "Gib mir . . . Schöpfung" reflects "dichter werden" of the fourth stanza, while the final "gib!" is the culmination of the poet's entreaty for creativity.

Yet the fourth part of the poem once again reverses the poet's mood as the depths of feeling give way to the heights of mental precision:

> "Bist du auf Grate gestiegen,
> sahst du die Gipfel klar;
> Adler, die wirklichen, fliegen
> schweigend und unfruchtbar."

The aqueous images of "Wasser und Welle" are replaced by lofty symbols of mountain peaks and eagles, which recall the "Formalist" and the "Himmel" of part II. Now once more Benn addresses himself critically with *du*. "Grate," "gestiegen," and "Gipfel" are alliterated to indicate their association: "gestiegen" refers not only to the poet's ascent of the mountain ridges but also his upward glance toward

the summit of poetic perfection. "Klar" is in opposition to
"Rausch" and the confused "hin und her" of the river flowing below. As disclosed already in part II, the "Denker"
exists in a world of silence: ". . . du trägst durch Nacht und
Schweigen / den Denker—ihn." "Unfruchtbar" indicates the
poet's aloofness from the organic processes of life. In his
essay "Altern als Problem für Künstler" (1954) Benn refers to
modern European artists as a "bio-negative assembly"
(1134). The artist exists in a sterile, ethereal realm, away
from men who fall short of perfection. In his "Über die
Krise der Sprache" (1934) Benn uses the image of the eagle
to contrast the artist with the normal man: "Der Mensch
ist ein Wesen, dessen Schöpfung nur ein halber Erfolg war.
Er ist nur ein Entwurf von etwas. Ein Adler war gedacht:
die Federn und Flügel waren bereits skizziert, aber die
ganze Form wurde nicht vollendet" (1718).

The second stanza continues to contrast organic life to
that which is "unfruchtbar":

> "Kürzer steht es in Früchten,
> früher, dass es verblich,
> nahe am Schöpfer züchten
> wenige Arten sich."

As earlier in the poem, where the artist must forsake the
grape harvest and bacchanalian songs of the summer, here
too the realm of art must segregate itself from organic life.
Benn writes in "Pallas":

> Das, was lebt, ist etwas anderes als das, was denkt. Dies ist
> eine fundamentale Tatsache von heute, wir müssen uns mit
> ihr abfinden. . . . Nicht nur abfinden: anerkennen . . . die
> Welt als spirituelle Konstruktion, als transzendentale Apper-
> zeption, die Existenz als geistigen Aufbau, das Sein als einen
> Traum von Form. . . . Es nähert sich das Gesetz der Kälte,
> der geringen Gemeinschaft. (927–28)

Yet few artists can approach the creator of such perfection:
"nahe am Schöpfer züchten wenige Arten sich." "Sich züch-

ten" stresses the aloofness of the artist's sphere from life: breeding or cultivation is emphasized rather than unrestricted growth. Benn comments in his "Doppelleben" (1943):

> Der Kunstträger ist statistisch asozial, lebt nur mit seinem inneren Material, er ist ganz uninteressiert an Verbreitung, Flächenwirkung, Aufnahmesteigerung, an Kultur. Er ist kalt, das Material muss kaltgehalten werden, er muss ja die Idee, die Wärme, denen sich die anderen menschlich überlassen dürfen, kalt machen, härten, dem weichen Stabilität verleihen. (2028)

"Ewig" at the beginning of the third stanza indicates the transcendental nature of the artistic realm: "schweigend" reiterates "schweigend und unfruchtbar" of the first stanza as well as "Nacht und Schweigen" of part II, thus emphasizing the detachment of the artistic world. "Das Blaue" represents the highest sphere of creative art. As Wodtke states, " 'Das Blaue' . . . has the same symbolic value as 'l'azur' for the French symbolists Baudelaire, Mallarmé and Valéry: it is identical with the coldness and absolute silence of empty space."[4]

The remainder of the third stanza contrasts "das Blaue" with the emotional "Tiefe" of parts I and III:

> ". . . wer noch an Stimmen denkt,
> hat schon den Blick, die Braue
> wieder in Sehnsucht gesenkt."

"Stimmen" opposes "schweigen" and suggests the activity, communication, and life denied to the ethereal artistic realm. The artist who does not maintain his austere devotion to form will lose his vision ("den Blick") of the figurative mountain peaks of perfection and be caught up in the transience of life. "Wieder in Sehnsucht" refers to the poet's longing described in the third quartet ("lass mich noch einmal reich sein . . . lass mich noch einmal weich sein . . ."), as well as to "das Verlangen zum Urgestein" in the second. "Gesenkt" concerns not only the poet's downward glance from the mountain region, but also suggests his immersion, and hence extinction, in the "Tiefe" of the river of life below (previously implied with "bis ihre Häupter *sanken . . .*" and "vor keiner Macht zu *sinken . . .*"). The stanza is highly musical, reflecting the emotion of life, yet it is not musical in overt images as before ("Weingesänge," "Schalmein," "singt man") but in its alliterative and assonantal *s*, *b*, and *w* sounds: "*s*chweigend / *S*timmen / *s*chon / *S*ehn*s*ucht / ge*s*enkt . . . *B*laue / *B*lick / *B*raue . . .*Ew*ig / *s*ch*w*eigend / *w*er / *w*ieder." The stanza is also comprised of deep, long vowels, which aurally promote the mood of "Sehnsucht."

The fourth stanza opposes these musical voices that seek to lull the poet into acquiescence. "Gestalten" implies form rather than emotion. "Du aber" introduces the contrast to the preceding stanza:

> "du aber dienst Gestalten
> über dem Brückenwehr
> über den stumpfen Gewalten
> Völker und Schnee und Meer."

The "Gestalten" exist in a transcendental region to which the "Formalist" aspires. They stand above the insensible forces ("stumpfen Gewalten") of society and nature ("Völker und Schnee und Meer"). The "Denker" is neither the shepherd nor the hunter of antiquity: he remains aloof from the historical process, because for him there is "kein Werden." He is impervious to natural forces in his effort to achieve immortality ("*Ewig* schweigend das Blaue"). "Schnee" reflects the colorless, insipid "stumpfe Gewalten." "Meer" is that to which the river of life flows and hence a symbol of the biological extinction that the poet must overcome.

The subsequent stanzas provide a final imperative for the artist, one related to the end of part II of the poem:

> "formen, das ist deine Fülle,
> der Rasse auferlegt,
> formen, bis die Hülle
> die ganze Tiefe trägt, . . ."

The poet's task of creating perfect forms is now seen as one that also nurtures depth and fullness. The forms that he creates are not individual to him alone but are characteristic of the whole Western civilization of which he is part ("du bist der Formenpräger der weissen Spur"). "Fülle" is the same fullness that the poet begged for at the conclusion of part III ("gib mir die Tiefe, die Fülle . . ."), yet no longer is the superficiality of form a hellish curse ("nimm mir die Hölle, die Hülle"). There is now an integration of inner and outer spheres, which eliminates all antitheses and thus brings about the perfect work of art ("formen, bis die Hülle / die ganze Tiefe trägt . . ."). Balser explains:

> Traum und Rausch können für sich selbst nicht bestehen, und eben deshalb ist der Künstler aufgerufen, die endogenen Bilder der mystischen Partizipation in die Statik und Abgeschlossenheit der Form zu überführen, bis sie "die ganze Tiefe trägt."[5]

"Form," "Tiefe," "Fülle," and "Hülle" are thus the "Elemente" constituting the "neue Macht" that Benn glimpses in the river at the beginning of the poem, but that he had been unable to comprehend.

The final stanza of the poem completes the synthesis of opposites:

> ". . die Hülle wird dann zeigen,
> und keiner kann entfliehn,
> dass Form und Tiefe Reigen,
> durch den die Adler ziehn."

"Hülle" is no longer merely an integument, but combines "Form" and "Tiefe" to become a "Reigen," a symbol of completion. As Benn states in "Altern als Problem für Künstler": "Die Kunst muss die Mitte wiederherstellen, aber sie muss auch die Tiefe nicht verlieren—die Kunst muss den Menschen als das Ebenbild Gottes darstellen—. . . ." (1136). In his "Rede auf Heinrich Mann" (1931) he similarly states, "Die neue Kunst, die Artistik, die nachnietzschesche Epoche, wo immer sie gross wurde, wurde es erkämpft aus der Antithese aus Rausch und Zucht." (980) "Reigen" now represents an emancipation from the confining "Ringen" at the beginning of the poem. "Ringen" and "Reigen" are both circular forms, yet "Reigen," a round dance, suggests music and celebration, which "Ringen" does not. Now the poet is no longer constricted within reality but has found the fulfillment and harmony he sought in "der neuen Macht." No longer is he an object of persecution as in part II ("und keinem du entfliehen . . .") but is integrated into the harmony of which everyone is part ("keiner kann entfliehen"). The repeated image of the eagles ("durch den die Adler ziehn") balances the "Tiefe" of the preceding verse ("dass Form und Tiefe Reigen . . .") and provides final emphasis for the poet, who exists "nahe am Schöpfer."

Throughout the poem the bridge represents a significant symbol of transition as well as union. As a symbol of transition it reflects Benn's rejection of his old National Socialistic allegiance and his consequent embracement of art. Transition is also seen in Benn's shift from the real world of "Ringe" to the harmony and fulfillment of art in "Reigen." In conjunction with the river, the bridge becomes a symbol for the organic transition from life to death that the "Formalist" must overcome. As a symbol of union the bridge reflects the junction connecting "Form" and "Tiefe." It is in his position on the bridge that the poet is able to discover a coalescence of extremes whereby thesis and antithesis are reconciled in a bridgelike synthesis at the end of the poem. The "neue Macht" that Benn glimpses from the bridge is thus clarified as an anticipation of his future work as a poet.

Appendix

A list (by title or first line) of poems in which the bridge symbol appears that are not used for discussion.

ANACKER, HEINRICH:
   "Seebrücke im Sturm"
BACHMANN, INGEBORG
   "Das Spiel ist aus"
BECKER, JOHANNES
   "Stadt mit Brücke"
BENRATH, HENRY
   "Basel"
   "Die Stadt"
DEHMEL, RICHARD
   "Die stille Stadt"
EICH GÜNTHER
   "Ende eines Sommers"
FREILIGRATH, FERDINAND
   "Die Seufzerbrücke"
FRIED, ERICH
   "Die Vogelbrücke"
GAN, PETER
   "Die Brücke"
HEISSENBÜTTEL, HELMUT
   "Topographie b"

HEYM, GEORG
    "Berlin"
    "Die Dämonen der Städte"
    "Die Heimat der Toten"
    "Schwarze Visionen"
HÖLDERLIN, FRIEDRICH
    "Patmos"
HÖLLERER, WALTER
    "Gaspard"
HOFMANNSTHAL, HUGO VON
    "Vor Tag"
    "Wir gingen einen Weg"
    "Leben, Traum und Tod . . ."
HUCH, RICARDA
    "Venedig"
JONAS, ERASMUS
    "Elemente"
KASACK, HERMANN
    "Gotische Brücke"
KELLER, GOTTFRIED
    "Der Waadländer Schild"
KLESSMANN, ECKART
    "Gesang von den Trommeln"
LILIENCRON, DETLEV VON
    "Auf einer Brücke"
MENZEL, HERBERT
    "Die Zugbrücke"
MIEGEL, AGNES
    "Heimweh"
MÖRIKE, EDUARD
    "Der Feuerreiter"
    "An Frau Pauline v. Phull-Rieppur auf Ober-Moensheim"
MOMBERT, ALFRED
    "Ich sass wohl einst auf einer hohen Brücke . . ."
    "Zehnter Denker: Die Brücke"
NIETZSCHE, FRIEDRICH
    "Nur Narr! Nur Dichter!"
PLATEN, AUGUST GRAF von
    "Wie rafft' ich mich auf . . ."
    "Mein Auge liess das hohe Meer zurücke, . . ."
    "Dies Labyrinth von Brücken und von Gassen . . ."

POINTEK, HEINZ
"Brückenromanze"
"Unter der Eisenbahnbrücke"
POLITZER, HEINZ
"Schlaflied unter der Brücke"
"Die Brücke"
REINIG, CHRISTA
"Der Enkel trinkt"
RÜCKERT, FRIEDRICH
"Die Scheidungsbrücke"
SCHNEIDER, REINHOLD
"Das Zeichen"
SCHOLZ, WILHELM VON
"Die Felsenbrücke"
"Brücken-Inschrift"
SCHRODER, RUDOLF ALEXANDER
"Die Brücke"
SPITTELER, CARL
"Das Brückengespenst"
"Die beiden Züge"
STRUB, URS MARTIN
"Gemini"
WEINHEBER, JOSEPH
"Die Brücke Blut, die zwischen Weib und Mann . . ."
"Brücken schlagen . . ."
WOLF, FRIEDRICH
"Auf der Brücke" (1944)
ZECH, PAUL
Die Eiserne Brücke (1913)
   1. "Bahnfahrt"
   2. "Der Hafen"
   3. "Die andere Stadt"
   4. "Die nüchterne Stadt"
ZERKAULEN, HEINRICH
"Die Brücke"

Notes

1 INTRODUCTION

1. C. J. Bleeker, "Die religiöse Bedeutung der Brücke," *Studies in the History of Religions* 7 (1963): 180–89.

2. Rudolf Erckmann, "Bahn, Brücke, Tunnel: Eine Arbeitsreihe über Dichtung der Technik," *Deutschunterricht* 11 (1960): 61–78.

3. Paul Friedman, "The Bridge: A Study in Symbolism," *The Yearbook of Psychoanalysis* 9 (1953): 257–82.

4. "Hölderlin's Ode 'Heidelberg,'" *Germanic Review* 37 (1962): 159.

5. Elisabeth Frenzel, *Stoff-, Motiv- und Symbolforschung* (Stuttgart, 1963), p. 97.

6. Gertrud von le Fort, *Werke* (Stuttgart, 1956), p. 88.

Deutsches Leid

Schiffer, zieh fort die Brücke,
Du lockst mich nimmermehr an Bord,
Ich weiss von keinem Glücke,
Ich weiss von keinem Zufluchtsort.

Und ob sich draussen weiten
Noch Länder froh und gastbereit,
Und ihre Arme breiten
Wie fremder Mütter Lindigkeit:

Ich würde doch entbehren
Bei ihres reichen Tisches Brot,
Ich würde mich verzehren
Nach meiner Heimat bittrer Not,

Ich stünde doch in Ketten
Mitten im festlich hohen Saal,
Ich könnt' mich niemals retten
Vor meines Volkes Schuld und Qual.

7. David Friedrich Strauss, *Gedichte* (Bonn, 1911), p. 22.

Ermunterung
Fort mit deinem alten Laster!
Allen Missmut ausgefegt!
Für die Wunden, die es schlägt,
Reicht das Leben auch das Pflaster.

Riss der Strom hinweg die Brücke,
Mutig in den Kahn hinein!
Nahm die Kugel dir ein Bein,
Greife rüstig nach der Krücke!

8. *The Collected Poems of Hart Crane*, ed. Waldo Frank (New York, 1933), p. 55.

9. *The Letters of Hart Crane*, ed. Brom Weber (New York, 1952), p. 124.

10. *Goethes Werke*, ed. Benno von Wiese and Erich Trunz (Hamburg, 1963), 6:238.

11. *Nietzsche Werke*, ed. Giorgio Colli and Mazzino Montinari (Berlin, 1968), 6, 1:10–11.

12. *Nietzsche*, 6, 1:12.

13. *Nietzsche*, 6, 1:244.

14. *Franz Kafka: Gesammelte Werke, Das Schloss*, ed. Max Brod (New York, 1946), p. 9.

15. *Das Schloss*, p. 260.

16. *Werke, Der Prozess*, p. 269.

17. *loc. cit.*

18. *Werke, Erzählungen*, p. 68.

19. *Werke, Beschreibung eines Kampfes: Novellen, Skizzen, Aphorismen aus dem Nachlass*, pp. 113–14:

"Ich war steif und kalt, ich war eine Brücke, über einem Abgrund lag ich. Diesseits waren die Fussspitzen, jenseits die Hände eingebohrt, in bröckelndem Lehm habe ich mich festgebissen. Die Schösse meines Rockes wehten zu meinen Seiten In der Tiefe lärmte der eisige Forellenbach. Kein Tourist verirrte sich zu dieser unwegsamen Höhe, die Brücke war in den Karten noch nicht eingezeichnet.—So lag ich und wartete; ich musste warten. Ohne einzustürzen kann keine einmal errichtete Brücke aufhören, Brücke zu sein.

Einmal gegen Abend war es war es der erste, war es der tausendste, ich weiss nicht,—meine Gedanken gingen immer in einem Wirrwarr und immer in der Runde. Gegen Abend im Sommer, dunkler rauschte der

Bach, da hörte ich einen Mannesschritt! Zu mir,—Strecke dich, Brücke, setze dich in Stand, geländerloser Balken, halte den dir Anvertrauten. Die Unsicherheit seines Schrittes gleiche unmerklich aus, schwankt er aber, dann gib dich zu erkennen und wie ein Berggott schleudere ihn ans Land. Er kam, mit der Eisenspitze seines Stockes beklopfte er mich, dann hob er mit ihr meine Rockschösse und ordnete sie auf mir. In mein buschiges Haar fuhr er mit der Spitze und liess sie, wahrscheinlich wild umherblickend, lange drin liegen. Dann aber—gerade träumte ich ihm nach über Berg und Tal—sprang er mit beiden Füssen mir mitten auf den Leib. Ich erschauerte in wildem Schmerz, gänzlich unwissend. Wer war es? Ein Kind? Ein Traum? Ein Wegelagerer? Ein Selbstmörder? Ein Versucher? Ein Vernichter? Und ich drehte mich um, ihn zu sehen. —Brücke dreht sich um! Ich war nicht umgedreht, da stürzte ich schon, ich stürzte, und schon war ich zerrissen und aufgespiesst von den zugespitzten Kieseln, die mich immer so friedlich aus dem rasenden Wasser angestarrt hatten."

20. *Thomas Mann Werke, Die Erzählungen* (Frankfurt am Main, 1967), 1:233.

21. Ibid., 1:20.

22. Ibid., 1:396.

23. *Werke, Der Zauberberg* 1:124.

24. Ibid., 1:126–27.

25. *Hermann Hesse: Gesammelte Dichtungen* (Suhrkamp Verlag, 1952), 3:143.

26. *Dichtungen,* 1:524.

2 FRIEDRICH HÖLDERLIN: "HEIDELBERG"

1. *Hölderlin: Sämtliche Werke,* ed. Friedrich Beissner (Stuttgart, 1951), 3:9. Hereafter cited as *Werke*.

2. *Hölderlins Sämtliche Werke,* ed. Ludwig V. Pigenot (Berlin, 1922), 3:245.

3. Mörike's letter to Hartlaub, March 26, 1847.

4. *Werke,* 2, 2:407–8.

5. Ibid., 408–13.

6. Ibid., 3:147.

7. Ibid., 1, 1:202–3.

8. In an earlier version of the poem Hölderlin suggests *Wipfel* with the following context of *Eichengipfel*:

> Wie der Vogel des Walds über die wehenden
> Eichengipfel so schwingt über den Strom. . . .

(*Werke,* 2, 2: 410).

9. Lawrence Ryan sees this depiction of the bridge as freedom within

form, "—denn diese Brücke verkörpert eine Beweglichkeit, die in einer dauernden Gestalt festghalten ist, ein 'Festgesetztes' also, in dem das 'Freie' noch fühlbar ist." *Hölderlins Lehre vom Wechsel der Töne* (Stuttgart, 1960), p. 186.

10. *Werke*, 1, 1 : 205.

11. Ibid., p. 207.

12. Johannes Klein, *Geschichte der deutschen Lyrik* (Wiesbaden, 1960), p. 408.

13. *Werke*, 2, 2 : 410.

14. Adolf Beck, " 'Heidelberg.' Versuch einer Deutung." *Hölderlin Jahrbuch* (1947), p. 52.

15. "Der Rhein" (*Werke*, 1, 2 : 144)
        . . . wie Bezauberte fliehn
    Die Wälder ihm nach und zusammensinkend die Berge.
"Der Nekar" (*Werke*, 1, 2 : 17)
        . . . Der Berge Quellen eilten hinab zu dir,
        Mit ihnen auch mein Herz und du nahmst uns mit,
            Zum stillerhabnen Rhein, zu seinen
                Städten hinunter und lustgen Inseln.

16. *Werke*, 1, 1 : 240.

17. "Die Heimat" (*Werke*, 1, 2 : 19) also emphasizes this bittersweet condition of man :
        Denn sie, die uns das himmlische Feuer leihn
        Die Götter schenken heiliges Leid uns auch,
            Drum bleibe dies. Ein Sohn der Erde
                Schein' ich; zu lieben gemacht, zu leiden.

18. *Werke*, 1, 1 : 201.

19. Staiger supports this view : with the castle the gods provide the river with an admonition not to relinquish itself, for the gods desire that mortals "lang im Lichte sich freun." Emil Staiger, "Heidelberg," *Meisterwerke der deutschen Sprache im 19. Jahrhundert* (Zürich, 1948), p. 23.

20. *Werke*, 3 : 150.

21. "Der Rhein" suggests that without man's existence and suffering, the realm of the gods would be without significance :
        Es haben aber an eigner
        Unsterblichkeit die Götter genug, und bedürfen
        Die Himmlischen eines Dings,
        So sinds Heroën und Menschen
        Und Sterbliche sonst.

22. H. A. Korff, *Geist der Goethezeit* (Leipzig, 1940), 3 : 399.

23. *Werke*, 1, 1 : 207.

24. Ibid., p. 205.

25. Ryan (*Wechsel der. Töne*, p. 188) comments on this harmony : "Das allzu Flüchtige des Stromes so wie das allzu Starre des Schlosses, beides von der lebendig ausgeglichenen Ruhe des Ganzen abweichend, werden in ihrer Einseitigkeit überwunden und in eine umfassende Harmonie einbezogen."

26. H. A. Korff, *Geist der Goethezeit*, 3:401.

27. Klein, *Geschichte*, p. 408.

28. "Hölderlin's Ode 'Heidelberg,'" *Germanic Review* 37 (1962):159. Silz remarks on the permanence of the final picture as being the unifying essence of the poem: "Its main theme, therefore, is the loveliness of something abiding, not the tragedy of something transient." Silz sees this permanence as the classical element of the poem and of Hölderlin's work in general.

29. *Werke*, 3:160.

30. Ibid., 1, 1:201.

31. Ibid., p. 208.

3 AUGUST GRAF VON PLATEN: "WENN TIEFE SCHWERMUT MEINE SEELE WIEGET . . ."

1. August Platen, *Tagebücher*, ed. L. von Laubmann and L. von Scheffler (Berlin, 1909), p. 183.

2. Ibid. p. 183

3. Ibid., p. 194.

4. Ibid., p. 176.

5. Theodor Schultz, *Platens Venedig-Erlebnis* (Berlin, 1940), p. 104.

6. Walther Naumann, in *Traum und Tradition in der deutschen Lyrik* (Kohlhammer, 1966), p. 151, asserts that the images of the second stanza are superfluous to the poem ("unnötige Erweiterungen"). On the contrary, they enforce the image structure of decay and desolation that characterize the poet's melancholia.

7. Heinrich Henel relates that Platen would often amuse himself by comparing himself to Homer and crowning himself with laurel wreaths. Heinrich Henel, *August von Platen: Gedichte* (Stuttgart, 1968), p. 168.

8. "Ein Lorbeerbusch ist ein in Venedig seltener, aber um so stärkerer Anblick." Johannes Klein, *Geschichte der deutschen Lyrik* (Wiesbaden, 1960), p. 662.

9. "Am Himmelfahrtstag fuhr der Doge unter grossen Feierlichkeiten im Bucentaur aufs Meer, um durch Versenken eines Ringes die 'Vermählung Venedigs mit der Adria zu vollziehen." August von Platen, *Dichtungen*, ed. Günther Voigt (Berlin, 1957), p. 226.

10. Klein, *Geschichte*, p. 662.

11. Emil Ermatinger, *Die deutsche Lyrik seit Herder* (Berlin, 1925), 2:243.

12. Philipp Witkop, *Die deutschen Lyriker* (Berlin, 1921), 2:124.

13. Hans Horst Lewald, *Platens geistiges Bild* (Essen, 1968), p. 37.

14. Ibid., pp. 41–42.

15. Platen's lack of stability is partially explained by his homoerotic inclinations, which plagued him from early youth. Unfortunately these

inclinations remained unreciprocated, and the consequent frustration often resulted in extreme depression and suicidal tendencies. (See Henel, pp. 154–55.) One might go so far as to say that Platen dwells on the decay of the city because it manifests the illness of his own mental condition. His unreciprocated, homoerotic tendencies resulted in a longing for death:

> Weil ich Liebe für so manche nährte,
> Glaubt ich töricht an Erwiderung;
> Spott nur wurde meinem geist'gen Streben,
> Und dem Streben meiner Seele Spott:
> O betaue dies verwelkte Leben . . . !

16. Klein, *Geschichte*, p. 515. The bridge symbol likewise figures significantly in several other poems in Platen's *Sonnette aus Venedig*:

1. "Wie rafft' ich mich auf in der Nacht, in der Nacht, . . ."
2. "Mein Auge liess das hohe Meer zurücke, . . ."
3. "Dies Labyrinth von Brücken und von Gassen, . . ."

4 CONRAD FERDINAND MEYER: "DIE ALTE BRÜCKE"

1. Johann Wolfgang von Goethe, *Goethes Werke in 14 Bänden* (Hamburg, 1966), 4:268.

2. Helene von Lerber, *Conrad Ferdinand Meyer* (Basel, 1949), p. 162.

3. Betsy Meyer, *Conrad Ferdinand Meyer. In der Erinnerung seiner Schwester Betsy Meyer* (Leipzig, 1903), p. 182.

4. Louis Wiesmann, *Conrad Ferdinand Meyer, Der Dichter des Todes und der Maske* (Bern, 1958), p. 154.

5. The bridge Meyer refers to is the old "Teufelsbrücke" over the Reuss in the Gotthard Pass. C. F. Meyer, *Werke*, ed. Hans Zeller and Alfred Zäch (Bern, 1967), 3:69.

6. In order to achieve this onomatopoeia, Meyer changed the original "Er *steigt* aus dumpfen Reussgetos." Heinrich Kraeger, *Conrad Ferdinand Meyer. Quellen und Wandlungen seiner Gedichte* (Berlin, 1901), p. 212.

7. Friedrich Theodor Vischer, *Kritische Gänge* (1844), p. 253.

8. *Werke*, 1:1868.

9. A similar event is experienced by Wulfrin in Meyer's novella *Die Richterin*: "Wulfrin gelangte an den Strom, der hier ohne Gewalt und Sturz Klippen und Felsen breit überflutete. Das Mondlicht verlockte ihn sich auf ein Felsstück zu lagern und wunsch- und schmerzlos mit den Wellen dahinzufliessen. *Er wurde sich selbst zum Traume.*" (Italics added) C. F. Meyer, *Werke*, 8:343.

10. Wiesmann, *Conrad Ferdinand Meyer*, p. 155.

11. Heinrich Henel, *The Poetry of Conrad Ferdinand Meyer* (Madison, Wis., 1954), p. 30.

12. Friedrich Theodore Vischer, *Auch Einer* (1844), p. 517.

13. Philipp Witkop, *Die deutschen Lyriker von Luther bis Nietzsche* (Berlin, 1921), 2:247.

14. "Auf Ponte Sisto" (see chap. 5) portrays a similar parade of historical figures.

15. Friedrich Schiller, Tell to Parricida in *Wilhelm Tell* (Act V):
"Ihr steigt hinauf, dem Strom der Reuss entgegen, die wildes Laufes von dem Berge stürzt—. . . Und seid ihr glücklich durch die Schrekkensstrasse, so kommt ihr auf die *Brücke, welche stäubet.*" (Italics added)

16. Meyer frequently uses the Alpine region as a symbol of the joining of north and south. Max Nussberger comments: "Meyers Reisen fassen das Engadin als Grenzgebiet des Nordens und Südens und lassen die Kennzeichen der verschiedenen Zonen als Gegensätze aufeinanderstossen, bald um ergründender Selbstbetrachtung zu nehmen." Max Nussberger, *Conrad Ferdinand Meyer, Leben und Werke* (Frauenfeld, 1919), p. 77.

17. *Briefe Conrad Ferdinand Meyers. Nebst seinen Recensionen und Aufsätzen,* ed. Adolf Frey (1916), p. 408. In a review by Meyer of Felix Dahn's poetry.

18. Quoted by Zeller in *Werke,* 3:69.

19. Helene von Lerber, *Conrad Ferdinand Meyer,* pp. 156–57.

20. Walther Linden, *Conrad Ferdinand Meyer: Entwicklung und Gestalt* (Munich, 1922), p. 225.

21. Henel, *The Poetry of C. F. Meyer,* p. 64.

22. Louis Wiesmann, *Conrad Ferdinand Meyer,* p. 51, refers in this respect to the "heidnische Gedanken" contained in the poem. But Meyer does not reject the notion of God; he modifies it to his own purposes.

23. *Werke,* 1:113.

24. Wiesmann, p. 153.

25. Ibid., p. 153.

26. Linden, *Conrad Ferdinand Meyer,* p. 207.

27. Ibid., p. 225.

28. Helene von Lerber, *Conrad Ferdinand Meyer,* p. 162.

29. Harry Maync, *Conrad Ferdinand Meyer und sein Werk* (Frauenfeld and Leipzig, 1925), p. 382.

30. Johannes Klein, *Geschichte der deutschen Lyrik* (Wiesbaden, 1960), p. 619.

31. Witkop, *Die deutschen Lyriker,* 2:246.

5 CONRAD FERDINAND MEYER: "AUF PONTE SISTO"

1. A similar seeking of the depths within the self and retreat from the light world is found in many poems by Meyer, notably "Eingelegte Ruder": "Unter mir—ach, aus dem Licht verschwunden— / Träumen schon die schönern meiner Stunden."

2. *The Poetry of Conrad Ferdinand Meyer* (Madison, Wis., 1954), pp. 31–32.

3. Betsy Meyer, *Conrad Ferdinand Meyer. In der Erinnerung seiner Schwester Betsy Meyer* (Leipzig, 1903),) p. 163.

4. C. F. Meyer, *Werke*, ed. Hans Zeller and Alfred Zäch (Bern, 1967), 1 : 354.

5. Betsy Meyer, *Conrad Ferdinand Meyer*, p. 162.

6. *Gedichte Conrad Ferdinand Meyers. Wege ihrer Vollendung*, ed. Heinrich Henel (Tübingen, 1962), p. 95.

7. *The Poetry of Conrad Ferdinand Meyer*, p. 169.

8. Ibid., p. 4.4

9. *Gedichte Conrad Ferdinand Meyers. Wege ihrer Vollendung*, p. 95–96.

10. Betsy Meyer, *Conrad Ferdinand Meyer*, p. 167.

11. *Werke*, 1 : 128.

6 THEODOR FONTANE: "DIE BRÜCK AM TAY"

1. *Zürcherische Freitagszeitung*, no. 1, January 2, 1880.

2. Ibid., no. 2, January 9, 1880.

3. "Die Landschaftsschilderung hat nur noch Wert, . . . wenn sie den Zweck verfolgt, Stimmungen vorzubereiten oder zu steigern. Das Muster auch hierfür ist Shakespeare. . . ." Theodor Fontane, *Sämtliche Werke*, ed. Edgar Gross and Kurt Schreinert (Munich, 1962), 1 : 40.

4. Fritz Martini, "Die Brück am Tay" in *Wege zum Gedicht*, ed. R. Hirschenauer and A. Weber (Munich, 1963), 2 : 385, questions the origin of this refrain: "Balladesk mehrdeutig ist dieser Abschluss; denn wird er wirklich noch von diesen Stimmen gesprochen? Ist er von dem Dichter gesprochen? Entstammt er einer anderen Stimme, die über allem, was hier laut wird und geschieht, das letzte schicksalhafte Resultat zieht?"

5. Kurt Bräutigam, *Die deutsche Ballade* (Frankfurt am Main, 1966), p. 113.

6. Martini, "Die Brück am Tay," p. 389.

7 FRIEDRICH NIETZSCHE: "VENEDIG"

1. Friedrich Nietzsche, *Ecce Homo, Nietzsche Werke*, ed. Giorgio Colli and Mazzino Montinari (Berlin, 1969), 5, 3 : 283. All Nietzsche quotations are from this edition.

2. *Ecce Homo* (1969), 6, 3 : 261.

3. *Also sprach Zarathustra* (1968), 6, 1 : 397.

4. August Langen, *Der Wortschatz des deutschen Pietismus* (Tübingen, 1954), p. 37.

5. Johannes Klein, *Die Dichtung Nietzsches* (Munich, 1936), p. 866, comments: "Von Musik ist nicht nur die Rede, sondern die Sprache selber wird zur Musik. . . . Das Erlebnis bildet sich in den Tönen ab und schafft bisher unerhörte Gesetzmässigkeiten."
6. *Ecce Homo*, 6, 3:289.
7. *Also sprach Zarathustra*, 6, 1:268.
8. Walter Kaufmann, *Nietzsche: Philosopher, Psychologist, Antichrist* (New York, 1959), p. 57.
9. W. D. Williams, "Nietzsche and Lyric Poetry," *Reality and Creative Vision* (London, 1963), p. 86, makes a comparison to Heine, who also destroys the idyllic moment that he creates: "It is not difficult to see general affinities between Nietzsche and Heine and to understand Nietzsche's admiration for the 'gay science' of Heine, the refusal to be committed, the sovereign play, the Voltairean freedom of the spirit, and of course the continual unmasking of humbug and pretence."
10. Johannes Klein, *Die Geschichte der deutschen Lyrik* (Wiesbaden, 1957), p. 663.
11. *Also sprach Zarathustra*, 6, 1:339.
12. Ibid., pp. 340–41.
13. *Der Wanderer und sein Schatten* (Berlin, 1967), 4, 3:328.
14. *Dionysos-Dithyramben* (1969), 6, 3:375.
15. *Also sprach Zarathustra*, 6, 1:10—11.

8 RAINER MARIA RILKE: "PONT DU CARROUSEL"

1. Rainer Maria Rilke, *Gesammelte Briefe*, ed. Walter Ritzer (Leipzig, 1930), 4:80.
2. Rainer Maria Rilke, *Tagebücher aus der Frühzeit* (Leipzig, 1942), p. 153. Letter of 10 March 1899.
3. The figure of the blind man is frequently used by Rilke. In "Das Lied des Blinden" the blind man alone lives and suffers within his inner realm:
    "Ihr draussen rührt euch und rückt und bildet euch ein,
    anders zu klingen als Stein auf Stein,
    aber ihr irrt euch: ich allein
    lebe und leide und lärme." (Rainer Maria Rilke, *Gesammelte Werke* [Leipzig, 1930], 2:174.)
In "Der Blinde" his sensitivity is emphasized:
    "Nur sein Fühlen rührt sich, so als finge
    es die Welt in kleinen Wellen ein. . . ." (*Werke*, 3:174.)
A short verse play, "Der Blinde," reveals the blind man as isolated but rich in spirit:
    Der Blinde:
    Ich bin eine Insel und allein.

Ich bin reich.—
Jetzt geht alles in mir umher,
sicher und sorglos; wie Genesende
gehn die Gefühle, geniessend des Gehn,
durch meines Leibes dunkles Haus.

(*Werke*, 2 : 156–58)

4. Quoted by Erich Simenauer, *Rainer Maria Rilke, Legende und Mythos* (Bern, 1953), p. 158, from an unpublished letter.

5. *Briefe 1902–1906*, No. 43, p. 109.

6. Also in Rilke's poem "Die Frucht" the fruit appears as "der Mittelpunkt" (*Werke*, 2 : 94):

Die Frucht

Das stieg zu ihr aus Erde, stieg und stieg,
und war verschwiegen in dem stillen Stamme
und wurde in der klaren Blüte Flamme,
bis es sich wiederum verschwieg.

Und fruchtete durch eines Sommers Länge
in dem bei Nacht und Tag bemühten Baum,
und kannte sich als kommendes Gedränge
wider den teilnahmsvollen Raum.

Und wenn es jetzt im rundenden Ovale
mit seiner vollgewordnen Ruhe prunkt,
stürzt es, erzichtend, innen der Schale
zurück in seinen *Mittelpunkt*. (Italics added)

7. *Tagebücher aus der Frühzeit*, p. 153, of 10 March 1899.

8. "Die spanische Trilogie," *Werke*, 3 : 446.

9. *Briefe*, 1 : 377.

10. From an unpublished letter of 2 July 1914, in "Rainer Maria Rilke und der Krieg. Unveröffentlichte Briefe des Dichters," *Neue Zürcher Zeitung*, June 1, 1941, p. 3.

11. *Tagebücher aus der Frühzeit*, p. 242.

12. Quoted in Emil Gasser, *Grundzüge der Lebensanschauung Rainer Maria Rilkes* (Bern, 1925), p. 177. From Rilke's *Rodin-Buch*: "Was die Dinge auszeichnet, dieses Ganz-mit-sich-Beschäftigtsein . . ." (Essay from 1903).

13. *Briefe 1914–1921*, No. 114, p. 284.

14. *Briefe 1902–1906*, p. 35.

15. *Tagebücher aus der Frühzeit*, p. 242.

16. *Werke*, 2 : 180.

17. Ibid., p. 176.

18. Ibid., 3 : 402.

19. *Briefe 1902–1906*, No. 45. p. 116.

20. *Briefe 1907–1914*, No. 58, p. 128.

21. Simenauer, *Rainer Marie Rilke*, p. 156.

22. Novalis, *Schriften*, ed. J. Minor (Jena, 1907), 2:114, No. 16.

23. *Werke*, 3:290.

24. Ibid., p. 94.

25. *Schriften*, 3:155, No. 8.

26. Johannes Klein, *Geschichte der deutschen Lyrik* (Wiesbaden, 1960), p. 408. (Italics added)

9 ERNST STADLER
"FAHRT ÜBER DIE KÖLNER RHEINBRÜCKE BEI NACHT"

1. The poet is able to break out of the misery that previously confined him. This release is reflected in the title of the collection in which "Fahrt über die Kölner Rheinbrücke bei Nacht" appeared: *Aufbruch*. Ernst Stadler, *Dichtungen*, ed. K. L. Schneider (Hamburg, 1954), 1:150–84.

10 GOTTFRIED BENN: "AM BRÜCKENWEHR"

1. Else Buddeberg comments, " 'Am Brückenwehr' . . . ist sehr aufschlussreich für das, was grundsätzlich über das lyrische Ich von Benn gedacht worden ist; aufschlussreich auch über die Stimmung, in der er nach der Krise von 1933—1934 sich befindet." *Gottfried Benn* (Stuttgart, 1961), p. 248.

2. Gottfried Benn, "Lebensweg eines Intellektualisten," *Gesammelte Werke*, ed. Dieter Wellershoff (Wiesbaden, 1968), 8:1886. Subsequent quotations will be from this edition and page numbers will be noted in the text.

3. Harald Steinhagen, *Die statischen Gedichte von Gottfried Benn* (Stuttgart, 1969), p. 58.

4. *Gottfried Benn: Selected Poems*, ed. Friedrich Wilhelm Wodtke (London: Oxford University Press, 1970), p. 177.

5. Hans-Dieter Balser, *Das Problem des Nihilismus im Werke Gottfried Benns* (Bonn, 1965), p. 139.

SELECTED BIBLIOGRAPHY

1 INTRODUCTION

Primary sources:
Crane, Hart. *The Collected Poems of Hart Crane.* Edited by Waldo Frank. New York, 1933.
————. *The Letters of Hart Crane.* Edited by Brom Weber. New York, 1952.
Goethe, J. W. von. *Goethes Werke.* Edited by Benno von Wiese and Erich Trunz. 14 vols. Hamburg, 1963.
Hesse, Hermann. *Hermann Hesse: Gesammelte Dichtungen.* 6 vols. Berlin, 1952.
Kafka, Franz. *Gesammelte Werke.* Edited by Max Brod. 6 vols. New York, 1946.
le Fort, Gertrud von. *Werke.* Stuttgart, 1956.
Mann, Thomas. *Thomas Mann Werke.* 12 vols. Frankfurt am Main, 1967.
Nietzsche, Friedrich. *Nietzsche Werke.* Edited by Giorgio Colli and Mazzino Montinari. Berlin, 1968.
Strauss, David Friedrich. *Gedichte.* Bern, 1911.

Secondary sources:
Bleeker, C. J. "Die religiöse Bedeutung der Brücke." *Studies in the History of Religion* 7 (1963): 180–89.
Erckmann, Rudolf. "Bahn, Brücke, Tunnel: Eine Arbeitsreihe über Dichtung der Technik." *Deutschunterricht* 11 (1960): 61–78.
Frenzel, Elisabeth. *Stoff-, Motiv- und Symbolforschung.* Stuttgart, 1963.
Friedman, Paul. "The Bridge: A Study in Symbolism." *The Yearbook of Psychoanalysis* 4 (1953): 257–82.
Silz, Walter. "Hölderlin's Ode 'Heidelberg.'" *Germanic Review* 37 (1962): 153–60.

2 HÖLDERLIN: "HEIDELBERG"

Primary sources:
Hölderlin, Friedrich. *Sämtliche Werke.* Edited by Friedrich Beissner. 6 vols. Stuttgart, 1951.
————. *Hölderlins Sämtliche Werke.* Edited by Ludwig V. Pigenot. 6 vols. Berlin, 1922.

Mörike, Eduard. *Eduard Mörike: Briefe*. Edited by Friedrich Seebass. Tübingen, 1942.

Secondary sources:
Beck, Adolf. " 'Heidelberg.' Versuch einer Deutung." *Hölderlin Jahrbuch* 1 (1947): 47–61.
Guardini, Romono. *Hölderlin: Weltbild und Frömmigkeit*. Leipzig, 1939.
Kelletat, Alfred, ed. *Hölderlin: Beiträge zu seinem Verständnis in unserm Jahrhundert*. Tübingen, 1961.
Klein, Johannes, *Geschichte der deutschen Lyrik*. Wiesbaden, 1960.
Korff, H. A. *Geist der Goethezeit*. 5 vols. Leipzig, 1940.
Ryan, Lawrence. *Hölderlins Lehre vom Wechsel der Töne*, Stuttgart, 1960.
Silz, Walter. "Hölderlin's Ode 'Heidelberg.'" *Germanic Review* 37 (1962): 153–60.
Staiger, Emil. *Meisterwerke der deutschen Sprache im 19. Jahrhundert*. Zürich, 1948.

3 AUGUST VON PLATEN
"WENN TIEFE SCHWERMUT MEINE SEELE WIEGET . . ."

Primary sources:
Platen, August von. *Dichtungen*. Edited by Günther Voigt. Berlin, 1957.
———. *Tagebücher*. Edited by L. von Laubmann and L. von Sheffler. Berlin 1909.

Secondary sources:
Ermatinger, Emil. *Die deutsche Lyrik seit Herder*. 2 vols. Berlin, 1925.
Henel, Heinrich. *August von Platen: Gedichte*. Stuttgart, 1968.
Klein, Johannes. *Geschichte der deutschen Lyrik*. Wiesbaden, 1960.
Lewald, Hans Horst. *Platens geistiges Bild*. Essen, 1968.
Naumann, Walter. *Traum und Tradition in der deutschen Lyrik*. Kohlhammer, 1966.
Schultz, Theodor. *Platens Venedig-Erlebnis*. Berlin, 1940.
Stemplinger, Eduard. *Der Münchner Kreis*. Leipzig, 1933.
Unger, Rudolf. *Platen in seinem Verhältnis zu Goethe*. Berlin, 1903.
Witkop, Philipp. *Die deutschen Lyriker*. 2 vols. Berlin, 1921.

4 CONRAD FERDINAND MEYER: "DIE ALTE BRÜCKE"

Primary sources:
Goethe, J. W. von. *Goethes Werke.* Edited by Benno von Wiese and Erich Trunz. 14 vols. Hamburg, 1963.
Meyer, Conrad Ferdinand. *Werke.* Edited by Hans Zeller and Alfred Zäch. Bern, 1967–.
———. *Briefe Conrad Ferdinand Meyers. Nebst seinen Recensionen und Aufsätzen.* Edited by Adolf Frey, Leipzig, 1908.

Secondary sources:
Brecht, Walther. *C. F. Meyer und das Kunstwerk seiner Gedichtsammlung.* Vienna and Leipzig, 1918.
Henel, Heinrich. *The Poetry of Conrad Ferdinand Meyer.* Madison, Wis., 1954.
Klein, Johannes. *Geschichte der deutschen Lyrik.* Wiesbaden, 1960.
Kraeger, Heinrich. *Conrad Ferdinand Meyer. Quellen und Wandlungen seiner Gedichte.* Berlin, 1901.
Lerber, Helene von. *Conrad Ferdinand Meyer: Der Mensch in der Spannung.* Basel, 1949.
Linden, Walther. *Conrad Ferdinand Meyer: Entwicklung und Gestalt.* Munich, 1922.
Maync, Harry. *Conrad Ferdinand Meyer und sein Werk.* Frauenfeld and Leipzig, 1925.
Meyer, Betsy. *Conrad Ferdinand Meyer. In der Erinnerung seiner Schwester Betsy Meyer.* Leipzig, 1903.
Pestalozzi, Karl. "Tod und Allegorie in C. F. Meyers Gedichten." *Euphorion* 56 (1962): 300–320.
Vischer, Friedrich T. *Auch Einer.* 1844.
Wiesmann, Louis. *Conrad Ferdinand Meyer: Der Dichter des Todes und der Maske.* Bern, 1958.
Witkop, Philipp. *Die deutschen Lyriker von Luther bis Nietzsche.* 2 vols. Berlin, 1921.

5 CONRAD FERDINAND MEYER: "AUF PONTE SISTO"

Primary sources:
Meyer, Conrad Ferdinand. *Werke.* Edited by Hans Zeller and Alfred Zäch. Bern, 1967–.

Secondary sources:
Henel, Heinrich. *Gedichte Conrad Ferdinand Meyers. Wege ihrer Vollendung.* Tübingen, 1962.
————. *The Poetry of Conrad Ferdinand Meyer.* Madison, Wis., 1954.
Meyer, Betsy. *Conrad Ferdinand Meyer. In der Erinnerung seiner Schwester Betsy Meyer.* Leipzig, 1903.

6 THEODOR FONTANE: "DIE BRÜCK AM TAY"

Primary sources:
Fontane, Theodor. *Sämtliche Werke.* Edited by Kurt Holbein. 27 vols. Munich, 1962.
Shakespeare, William. *The Works of Shakespeare.* Edited by W. Elwin. 16 vols. New York, 1959.

Secondary sources:
Bräutigam, Kurt. *Die deutsche Ballade.* Frankfurt am Main, 1965.
Ermatinger, Emil. *Die deutsche Lyrik seit Herder.* 3 vols. Leipzig and Berlin, 1925.
Hinck, Walter. *Die deutsche Ballade von Bürger bis Brecht.* Göttingen, 1968.
Hirschenauer, R., and Weber, A., eds. *Wege zum Gedicht.* 2 vols. Munich, 1963.

7 FRIEDRICH NIETZSCHE: "VENEDIG"

Primary sources:
Nietzsche, Friedrich. *Nietzsche Werke.* Edited by Giorgio Colli and Mazzino Montinari. Berlin, 1968–.

Secondary sources:
Hermand, Jost. "Nietzsche Gedichte: Nachwort." In *Nietzsche Gedichte,* edited by Jost Hermand, pp. 131–40. Stuttgart, 1974.
Kaufmann, Walter. *Nietzsche: Philosopher, Psychologist, Antichrist.* New York, 1959.
Langen, August. *Der Wortschatz des deutschen Pietismus.* Tübingen, 1954.

Klein, Johannes. *Die Dichtung Nietzsches.* Munich, 1936.
———. *Geschichte der deutschen Lyrik.* Wiesbaden, 1957.
Pütz, Peter. *Friedrich Nietzsche.* Stuttgart, 1967.
Williams, W. D. "Nietzsche and Lyric Poetry." In *Reality and Creative Vision,* edited by Albert Closs, pp. 85–100. London, 1963.
Witkop, Phillip. *Die deutschen Lyriker von Luther bis Nietzsche.* 2 vols. Berlin, 1921.

8   RAINER MARIA RILKE: "PONT DU CARROUSEL"

Primary sources:
Novalis, *Schriften.* Edited by J. Minor. 4 vols. Jena, 1907.
Rilke, Rainer Maria. *Gesammelte Werke.* Edited by Walter Ritzer. 6 vols. Leipzig, 1930.
———. *Gesammelte Briefe.* Edited by Walter Ritzer. 6 vols. Leipzig, 1930.

Secondary sources:
Bollnow, Otto Friedrich. *Rilke.* Stuttgart, 1951.
Buddeberg, Else. *Rainer Maria Rilke: Eine Innere Biographie.* Stuttgart, 1960.
Gasser, Emil. *Grundzüge der Lebensanschauung Rainer Maria Rilkes.* Bern, 1925.
Günther, Werner. *Weltinnenraum: Die Dichtung Rainer Maria Rilkes.* Leipzig, 1943.
Klein, Johannes. *Geschichte der deutschen Lyrik.* Wiesbaden, 1960.
Simenauer, Erich. *Rainer Maria Rilke: Legende und Mythos.* Bern, 1953.

9   ERNST STADLER:
"FAHRT ÜBER DIE KÖLNER RHEINBRÜCKE BEI NACHT"

Primary sources:
Stadler, Ernst. *Dichtungen.* Edited by Karl Ludwig Schneider. 2 vols. Hamburg, 1954.

Secondary sources:
Rölleke, Heinz. *Die Stadt bei Stadler, Heym, und Trakl.* Berlin, 1966.

Schirokauer, Arno. "Über Ernst Stadler." *Akzente* 1 (1954): 320–34.

Schneider, Karl Ludwig. *Der bildhafte Ausdruck in den Dichtungen Georg Heyms, Georg Trakls, und Ernst Stadlers.* Heidelberg, 1954.

Schumann, Detlev W. "Ernst Stadler and German Expressionism" *JEGP* 29 (1930): 510–34.

10 GOTTFRIED BENN: "AM BRÜCKENWEHR"

Primary sources:
Benn, Gottfried. *Gesammelte Werke.* Edited by Dieter Wellershoff. 8 vols. Wiesbaden, 1968.

———: *Gottfried Benn: Selected Poems.* Edited by Friedrich Wilhelm Wodtke. London: Oxford University Press, 1970.

Secondary sources:
Buddeberg, Else. *Gottfried Benn.* Stuttgart, 1961.

———. *Probleme um Gottfried Benn.* Stuttgart, 1962.

Balser, Hans-Dieter. *Das Problem des Nihilismus im Werke Gottfried Benns.* Bonn, 1965.

Hillebrand, Bruno. *Artistik und Auftrag: Zur Kunsttheorie von Benn und Nietzsche.* Munich, 1966.

Klein, Johannes. *Geschichte der deutschen Lyrik.* Wiesbaden, 1960.

Lennig, Walter. *Gottfried Benn.* Hamburg, 1962.

Wodtke, Friedrich Wilhelm. *Gottfried Benn.* Stuttgart, 1962.

Index